P9-CQQ-047

POCKET

Life List

A Birdwatcher's Life List and
Diary of North American Birds

BERNARD A. FASHINGBAUER

NAME

ADDRESS

CITY/STATE/ZIP

PHONE

DATE BEGUN

SYREN BOOK COMPANY
SAINT PAUL

Published by
Syren Book Company LLC
2402 University Avenue West
Saint Paul, Minnesota 55114

Printed in the United States of America on acid-free paper.

ISBN 0-929636-24-4

To order additional copies of this book see the order form
at the back of the book or www.itascabooks.com.

Contents

Introduction
v

Map of North America
xii

List of North American Birds (North of Mexico)
1

Bibliography
211

Index of Species
213

Introduction

Bird-watching is now Number One! With the possible exception of combined hunting and fishing sports, this absorbing pastime ranks first among worldwide hobbies, even surpassing stamp and coin collecting as the choice of millions.

Bird-watching as a hobby begins simply enough. You seek out birds, the more species the better, and repeated observations of the same species are not considered boring. Like many hobbies, it can be enhanced by travel and, better than most, it can be enjoyed almost any place on earth—usually at little or no additional cost. Furthermore, bird-watching can be enjoyed twenty-four hours a day any season of the year throughout much of the world, and it lends itself to both solo or group outings. It can be a pleasing, casual episode in the lives of many and may approach or even exceed fanaticism with more than a few. Thousands of observers limit their viewing to through-the-window and perhaps backyard feeding stations, whereas at the other extreme, growing numbers participate (usually for charitable fund-raising causes) in grueling long-distance "birding" marathons.

Birds, more so than other groups of animals, offer beauty and charm in the form of color, song, and fascinating behavioral traits. A few species can become a nuisance, but generally birds endear themselves to people of all ages. To experience the joy of this hobby, begin with this Pocket Life List. Record the various species that you discover around your home in the city or in the country, at local and national parks, on business and leisure travels—wherever you encounter birds!

Those whose avocational or professional training has already inspired systematic note-taking will require no prompting regarding the value of proper record-keeping. But I urge more casual novices to record their field notes carefully and thoroughly so that they may contribute to a fund of scientific knowledge. Information of this kind, when reliably gathered, becomes increasingly valuable in assessing the environmental quality of our nation and other regions of the world.

To make checklist records scientifically useful and to sustain your personal interest, consider entering the following types of information under each species' name: names of your companions; altitude in mountainous terrain; observed bird behavior such as calling, singing, flying, swimming, feeding, territorial defense, courtship and nest building; relative abundance; weather conditions; and whatever else you find personally fulfilling. As years pass, what you had regarded as commonplace may become history, and you will have helped write it! But perhaps of equal import, you will have experienced pleasant camaraderie likely to greatly enhance the remainder of your life.

Your Life List is almost certain to inspire you to seek greater birding and associated outdoor adventures. Soon you will want to accumulate a nature library, include photography in your outings and "stop and smell the flowers" as you creep up on a particularly unusual bird whose identity puzzles you. Birding is perhaps as close as you can come to a no-lose situation.

Tabulating birds observed is a "big thing" in the lives of many birders, and there are established lists for almost every conceivable occurrence or event. Included are tallies pertaining to backyard observations and other specific areas; counts extending over the period of a day, season or year; special events such as the national annual Christmas Bird Count; breeding bird census; first arrival dates in the spring; latest departure dates in the fall. Recently birding marathons have grown rapidly in popularity. For serious birders, the expression "Any excuse for a party" is parlayed into "Any excuse for a bird count."

To most birders the epitome of bird tallies is the Life List. The lengths to which some zealous birders will go to build their life lists merits the attention of even the international media. On a worldwide basis, the long sought numerical goal is the magic 7,000! Of some 8,600 to 9,000 species of birds believed to exist throughout the world, the greatest number recorded seen by any one person is reportedly 6,600. A select few birders are known to have reached 6,000 or more and are striving to exceed this extraordinary achievement. Relatively large sums of time and money have been spent in these intensive endeavors.

A more modest, but nonetheless exceptionally challenging, goal is the search for bird species to be found within North America north of Mexico. This region includes offshore islands and adjoining ocean areas generally limited to within 100 miles from the mainland. Approximately 850 species are known to occur here. An exact number is difficult to establish as official recognition of North American species, as with other regions of the world, remains in a state of flux. By 1985, according to the American Birding

Association (ABA), 439 birders had attained a listing of 600 or more species for this portion of North America. By 1986 one gentleman reached a lifetime listing of 760 North American birds! He headed an exclusive fraternity of less than 50 known members who reached or exceeded the astounding number of 700 species. These accomplishments are certain to increase with time.

Of course the tropical regions of the world host the majority of the known bird species, and the New World is exceptional in this regard. Over 1,600 species are found within several South American countries, and Mexico lists over 1,000. The species that stray over our common border with Mexico add much to the excitement of birding in the southwestern portions of the United States. West Indian species are occasionally discovered in and about Florida, and in the coastal areas of Alaska certain Asian species occur, albeit rarely.

SPECIES INCLUDED IN THIS CHECKLIST

Determining which species of birds to include in this checklist was complicated by indecisions involving several factors. The presence of erratic wanderers from Europe, Asia, Mexico and the Caribbean; intentionally introduced or escaped exotics; and far-ranging pelagic seabirds contributed to the confusion. Many of these "accidentals" are seen only rarely by a minute number of birders, but since they do occur, they invite inclusion in North America's list of avian species. The listing of a few birds in some checklists is based upon as little as a single sighting or two over a period of many years. The merit of including all of these over a region as vast as the northern portion of the North American continent remains questionable and is not easily resolved.

The two major North American checklists, A.O.U. (American Ornithologists Union) and ABA (American Birding Association), served as the basis for this checklist. The decision whether to include a certain introduced species or erratic migrant was tempered slightly with the recognition it was accorded by current avian journals and other ornithological literature. Final inclusion problems were resolved by favoring those erratic species described and/or illustrated in the more recent bird guides, as these form the basis of identification used by birders throughout North America.

The U.S./Mexico border was selected as the southern limit of geographic coverage chiefly for practical reasons, as the inclusion of Mexican and Central American species would have more than doubled the number of entries. Most of North America's tropical birds are customarily treated in separate field guides and checklists—and, following custom, this book does not include them.

CHECKLIST ORDER

The sequential arrangement of the species in this Life List is based upon the sixth edition of the A.O.U. checklist published in 1983. This authoritative listing considers the presumed phylogenetic or ancestral relationships among birds ranging from the most primitive to the most advanced. Periodic revisions of this sequence are made only after serious scientific study and contemplation. Resulting taxonomic changes occur as a result of both the "splitting" and "lumping" of bird species. However, such revisions are aggravating to many birders, and name deletions and changes, particularly, are met with some resistance. Fortunately, changes in the name more significantly affect the common or English name of a bird, and the Latin or scientific name remains a stable base for reference when changes occur in the vernacular nomenclature.

FIELD GUIDES AND ASSOCIATED IDENTIFICATION AIDS

Field guides are essential to the proper identification of birds and therefore of tremendous assistance in completing your Life List. An excellent assortment is available for even many of the more remote areas of the world, and field guides are especially thorough in the identification of North American birds. Some guides contain range maps which are of particular assistance to the amateur birder by eliminating from consideration species that occur rarely, if ever, within a specific region being studied.

Of course bird books of all kinds, including the large format monographs, regional studies and several periodic journals and magazines, are also useful to the birder. In addition, the many local checklists and both audio and video recordings will significantly assist in identifying many of the more common birds. Learning to identify birds by their songs and calls requires considerable practice, but it is a very effective means of discovery, particularly in heavy cover.

"How To" and "Where To" books referring to bird

watching can help the novice become a learned birder. Many tips and ideas set forth in these books are the result of countless hours spent by advanced birders doing exactly what the beginner must learn to become truly proficient in this hobby. Finally, becoming a member of a local bird club and perhaps a national society devoted to bird study will provide much current information and further your enjoyment appreciably.

GOOD BIRDING!

Throughout all your days afield, conduct yourself properly. Don't allow your enthusiasm to cause you to disregard the privacy and quiet of others. Be courteous to everyone, including fellow birders. Birding "ethics" are crucial to a continuation of the usual warm welcome bird watchers are offered worldwide.

Orders:

List of
North
American
Birds

*North of
Mexico*

A.O.U.
Check-list,
Sixth Edition

(*Species index
on page* 213)

GAVIIFORMES

PODICIPEDIFORMES

PROCELLARIIFORMES

PELECANIFORMES

CICONIIFORMES

PHOENICOPTERIFORMES

ANSERIFORMES

FALCONIFORMES

GALLIFORMES

GRUIFORMES

CHARADRIIFORMES

COLUMBIFORMES

PSITTACIFORMES

CUCULIFORMES

STRIGIFORMES

CAPRIMULGIFORMES

APODIFORMES

TROGONIFORMES

CORACIIFORMES

PICIFORMES

PASSERIFORMES

Loons (*Gaviidae*)

Red-throated Loon   *Gavia stellata*

DATE

LOCALITY

HABITAT

NOTES

Arctic Loon   *Gavia arctica*

DATE

LOCALITY

HABITAT

NOTES

Common Loon   *Gavia immer*

DATE

LOCALITY

HABITAT

NOTES

Yellow-billed Loon   *Gavia adamsii*

DATE

LOCALITY

HABITAT

NOTES

Grebes (*Podicipedidae*)

Least Grebe   *Tachybaptus dominicus*

DATE

LOCALITY

HABITAT

NOTES

Pied-billed Grebe   *Podilymbus podiceps*

DATE

LOCALITY

HABITAT

NOTES

Horned Grebe   *Podiceps auritus*

DATE

LOCALITY

HABITAT

NOTES

Red-necked Grebe   *Podiceps grisegena*

DATE

LOCALITY

HABITAT

NOTES

Eared Grebe   *Podiceps nigricollis*

DATE

LOCALITY

HABITAT

NOTES

Western Grebe   *Aechmophorus occidentalis*

DATE

LOCALITY

HABITAT

NOTES

Albatrosses (*Diomedeidae*)

P
R
O
C
E
L
L
A
R
I
I
F
O
R
M
E
S

Short-tailed Albatross   *Diomedea albatrus*

DATE

LOCALITY

HABITAT

NOTES

Black-footed albatross   *Diomedea nigripes*

DATE

LOCALITY

HABITAT

NOTES

Laysan Albatross   *Diomedea immutabilis*

DATE

LOCALITY

HABITAT

NOTES

Black-browed Albatross   *Diomedea melanophris*

DATE

LOCALITY

HABITAT

NOTES

Shy Albatross   *Diomedea cauta*

DATE

LOCALITY

HABITAT

NOTES

Yellow-nosed Albatross   *Diomedea chlororhynchos*

DATE

LOCALITY

HABITAT

NOTES

Fulmars, Shearwaters and Petrels
(Procellariidae)

Northern Fulmar   *Fulmarus glacialis*

DATE
....

LOCALITY
....

HABITAT
....

NOTES
....

Black-capped Petrel   *Pterodroma hasitata*

DATE
....

LOCALITY
....

HABITAT
....

NOTES
....

Mottled Petrel   *Pterodroma inexpectata*

DATE
....

LOCALITY
....

HABITAT
....

NOTES
....

Streaked Shearwater   *Calonectris leucomelas*

DATE
....

LOCALITY
....

HABITAT
....

NOTES
....

Cory's Shearwater — *Calonectris diomedea*

DATE

LOCALITY

HABITAT

NOTES

Pink-footed Shearwater — *Puffinus creatopus*

DATE

LOCALITY

HABITAT

NOTES

Flesh-footed Shearwater — *Puffinus carneipes*

DATE

LOCALITY

HABITAT

NOTES

Greater Shearwater — *Puffinus gravis*

DATE

LOCALITY

HABITAT

NOTES

Buller's Shearwater   *Puffinus bulleri*

DATE

LOCALITY

HABITAT

NOTES

Sooty Shearwater   *Puffinus griseus*

DATE

LOCALITY

HABITAT

NOTES

Short-tailed Shearwater   *Puffinus tenuirostris*

DATE

LOCALITY

HABITAT

NOTES

Manx Shearwater   *Puffinus puffinus*

DATE

LOCALITY

HABITAT

NOTES

Black-vented Shearwater *Puffinus opisthomelas*

DATE

LOCALITY

HABITAT

NOTES

Little Shearwater *Puffinus assimilis*

DATE

LOCALITY

HABITAT

NOTES

Audubon's Shearwater *Puffinus iherminieri*

DATE

LOCALITY

HABITAT

NOTES

Storm-Petrels (*Hydrobatidae*)

Wilson's Storm-Petrel *Oceanites oceanicus*

DATE

LOCALITY

HABITAT

NOTES

White-faced Storm-Petrel   *Pelagodroma marina*

DATE

LOCALITY

HABITAT

NOTES

British Storm-Petrel   *Hydrobates pelagicus*

DATE

LOCALITY

HABITAT

NOTES

Fork-tailed Storm-Petrel   *Oceanodroma furcata*

DATE

LOCALITY

HABITAT

NOTES

Leach's Storm-Petrel   *Oceanodroma leucorhoa*

DATE

LOCALITY

HABITAT

NOTES

Ashy Storm-Petrel *Oceanodroma homochroa*

DATE

LOCALITY

HABITAT

NOTES

Band-rumped Storm-Petrel *Oceanodroma castro*

DATE

LOCALITY

HABITAT

NOTES

Wedge-rumped Storm-Petrel *Oceanodroma tethys*

DATE

LOCALITY

HABITAT

NOTES

Black Storm-Petrel *Oceanodroma melania*

DATE

LOCALITY

HABITAT

NOTES

Least Storm-Petrel *Oceanodroma microsoma*

DATE

LOCALITY

HABITAT

NOTES

Tropicbirds (*Phaethontidae*)

White-tailed Tropicbird *Phaethon lepturus*

DATE

LOCALITY

HABITAT

NOTES

Red-billed Tropicbird *Phaethon aethereus*

DATE

LOCALITY

HABITAT

NOTES

Red-tailed Tropicbird *Phaethon rubricauda*

DATE

LOCALITY

HABITAT

NOTES

Boobies and Gannets (*Sulidae*)

Masked Booby — *Sula dactylatra*

DATE

LOCALITY

HABITAT

NOTES

Blue-footed Booby — *Sula nebouxii*

DATE

LOCALITY

HABITAT

NOTES

Brown Booby — *Sula leucogaster*

DATE

LOCALITY

HABITAT

NOTES

Red-footed Booby — *Sula sula*

DATE

LOCALITY

HABITAT

NOTES

Northern Gannet   *Sula bassanus*

DATE

LOCALITY

HABITAT

NOTES

Pelicans (*Pelecanidae*)

American White Pelican   *Pelecanus erythrorhynchos*

DATE

LOCALITY

HABITAT

NOTES

Brown Pelican   *Pelecanus occidentalis*

DATE

LOCALITY

HABITAT

NOTES

Cormorants (*Phalacrocoracidae*)

Great Cormorant   *Phalacrocorax carbo*

DATE

LOCALITY

HABITAT

NOTES

Double-crested Cormorant *Phalacrocorax auritus*

DATE

LOCALITY

HABITAT

NOTES

Olivaceous Cormorant *Phalacrocorax olivaceus*

DATE

LOCALITY

HABITAT

NOTES

Brandt's Cormorant *Phalacrocorax penicillatus*

DATE

LOCALITY

HABITAT

NOTES

Pelagic Cormorant *Phalacrocorax pelagicus*

DATE

LOCALITY

HABITAT

NOTES

Red-faced Cormorant   *Phalacrocorax urile*

DATE

LOCALITY

HABITAT

NOTES

Anhingas (*Anhingidae*)

Anhinga   *Anhinga anhinga*

DATE

LOCALITY

HABITAT

NOTES

Frigatebirds (*Fregatidae*)

Magnificent Frigatebird   *Fregata magnificens*

DATE

LOCALITY

HABITAT

NOTES

Great Frigatebird   *Fregata minor*

DATE

LOCALITY

HABITAT

NOTES

Lesser Frigatebird   *Fregata ariel*

DATE

LOCALITY

HABITAT

NOTES

Bitterns and Herons *(Ardeidae)*

American Bittern   *Botaurus lentiginosus*

DATE

LOCALITY

HABITAT

NOTES

Least Bittern   *Ixobrychus exilis*

DATE

LOCALITY

HABITAT

NOTES

Great Blue Heron   *Ardea herodias*

DATE

LOCALITY

HABITAT

NOTES

C
I
C
O
N
I
F
O
R
M
E
S

Great Egret   *Casmerodius albus*

DATE

LOCALITY

HABITAT

NOTES

Chinese Egret   *Egretta eulophotes*

DATE

LOCALITY

HABITAT

NOTES

Little Egret   *Egretta garzetta*

DATE

LOCALITY

HABITAT

NOTES

Snowy Egreet   *Egretta thula*

DATE

LOCALITY

HABITAT

NOTES

Little Blue Heron   *Egretta caerulea*

DATE

LOCALITY

HABITAT

NOTES

Tricolored Heron   *Egretta tricolor*

DATE

LOCALITY

HABITAT

NOTES

Reddish Egret   *Egretta rufescens*

DATE

LOCALITY

HABITAT

NOTES

Cattle Egret   *Bubulcus ibis*

DATE

LOCALITY

HABITAT

NOTES

Green-backed Heron   *Butorides striatus*

DATE

LOCALITY

HABITAT

NOTES

Black-crowned Night-Heron   *Nycticorax nycticorax*

DATE

LOCALITY

HABITAT

NOTES

Yellow-crowned Night-Heron   *Nycticorax violaceus*

DATE

LOCALITY

HABITAT

NOTES

Ibises and Spoonbills (*Threskiornithidae*)

White Ibis   *Eudocimus albus*

DATE

LOCALITY

HABITAT

NOTES

Scarlet Ibis   *Eudocimus ruber*

DATE

LOCALITY

HABITAT

NOTES

Glossy Ibis   *Plegadis falcinellus*

DATE

LOCALITY

HABITAT

NOTES

White-faced Ibis   *Plegadis chihi*

DATE

LOCALITY

HABITAT

NOTES

Roseate Spoonbill   *Ajaia ajaja*

DATE

LOCALITY

HABITAT

NOTES

Storks (*Ciconiidae*)

Jabiru   *Jabiru mycteria*

DATE

LOCALITY

HABITAT

NOTES

Wood Stork   *Mycteria americana*

DATE

LOCALITY

HABITAT

NOTES

Flamingos (*Phoenicopteridae*)

Greater Flamingo   *Phoenicopterus ruber*

DATE

LOCALITY

HABITAT

NOTES

Swans, Geese and Ducks (*Anatidae*)

Fulvous Whistling-Duck   *Dendrocygna bicolor*

DATE

LOCALITY

HABITAT

NOTES

Black-bellied Whistling-Duck
Dendrocygna autumnalis

DATE

LOCALITY

HABITAT

NOTES

Tundra Swan   *Cygnus columbianus*

DATE

LOCALITY

HABITAT

NOTES

Whooper Swan   *Cygnus cygnus*

DATE

LOCALITY

HABITAT

NOTES

Trumpeter Swan   *Cygnus buccinator*

DATE

LOCALITY

HABITAT

NOTES

Mute Swan *Cygnus olor*

DATE

LOCALITY

HABITAT

NOTES

Bean Goose *Anser fabalis*

DATE

LOCALITY

HABITAT

NOTES

Pink-footed Goose *Anser brachyrhynchus*

DATE

LOCALITY

HABITAT

NOTES

Lesser White-fronted Goose *Anser erythropus*

DATE

LOCALITY

HABITAT

NOTES

Greater White-fronted Goose   *Anser albifrons*

DATE

LOCALITY

HABITAT

NOTES

Snow Goose   *Chen caerulescens*

DATE

LOCALITY

HABITAT

NOTES

Ross' Goose   *Chen rossii*

DATE

LOCALITY

HABITAT

NOTES

Emperor Goose   *Chen canagica*

DATE

LOCALITY

HABITAT

NOTES

Brant   *Branta bernicla*

DATE

LOCALITY

HABITAT

NOTES

Barnacle Goose   *Branta leucopsis*

DATE

LOCALITY

HABITAT

NOTES

Canada Goose   *Branta canadensis*

DATE

LOCALITY

HABITAT

NOTES

Wood Duck   *Aix sponsa*

DATE

LOCALITY

HABITAT

NOTES

Green-winged Teal   *Anas crecca*

DATE

LOCALITY

HABITAT

NOTES

Baikal Teal   *Anas formosa*

DATE

LOCALITY

HABITAT

NOTES

Falcated Teal   *Anas falcata*

DATE

LOCALITY

HABITAT

NOTES

American Black Duck   *Anas rubripes*

DATE

LOCALITY

HABITAT

NOTES

Mottled Duck   *Anas Fulvigula*

DATE

LOCALITY

HABITAT

NOTES

Mallard   *Anas platyrhynchos*

DATE

LOCALITY

HABITAT

NOTES

Spot-billed Duck   *Anas poecilorhyncha*

DATE

LOCALITY

HABITAT

NOTES

White-cheeked Pintail   *Anas bahamensis*

DATE

LOCALITY

HABITAT

NOTES

Northern Pintail   *Anas acuta*

DATE

LOCALITY

HABITAT

NOTES

Garganey   *Anas querquedula*

DATE

LOCALITY

HABITAT

NOTES

Blue-winged Teal   *Anas discors*

DATE

LOCALITY

HABITAT

NOTES

Cinnamon Teal   *Anas cyanoptera*

DATE

LOCALITY

HABITAT

NOTES

Northern Shoveler   *Anas clypeata*

DATE

LOCALITY

HABITAT

NOTES

Gadwall   *Anas strepera*

DATE

LOCALITY

HABITAT

NOTES

Eurasian Wigeon   *Anas penelope*

DATE

LOCALITY

HABITAT

NOTES

American Wigeon   *Anas americana*

DATE

LOCALITY

HABITAT

NOTES

Common Pochard   *Aythya ferina*

DATE

LOCALITY

HABITAT

NOTES

Canvasback   *Aythya valisineria*

DATE

LOCALITY

HABITAT

NOTES

Redhead   *Aythya americana*

DATE

LOCALITY

HABITAT

NOTES

Ring-necked Duck   *Aythya collaris*

DATE

LOCALITY

HABITAT

NOTES

Tufted Duck   *Aythya fuligula*

DATE

LOCALITY

HABITAT

NOTES

Greater Scaup   *Aythya marila*

DATE

LOCALITY

HABITAT

NOTES

Lesser Scaup   *Aythya affinis*

DATE

LOCALITY

HABITAT

NOTES

Common Eider   *Somateria mollissima*

DATE

LOCALITY

HABITAT

NOTES

King Eider   *Somateria spectabilis*

DATE

LOCALITY

HABITAT

NOTES

Spectacled Eider   *Somateria fischeri*

DATE

LOCALITY

HABITAT

NOTES

Steller's Eider   *Polysticta stelleri*

DATE

LOCALITY

HABITAT

NOTES

Harlequin Duck   *Histrionicus histrionicus*

DATE

LOCALITY

HABITAT

NOTES

Oldsquaw *Clangula hyemalis*

DATE

LOCALITY

HABITAT

NOTES

Black Scoter *Melanitta nigra*

DATE

LOCALITY

HABITAT

NOTES

Surf Scoter *Melanitta perspicillata*

DATE

LOCALITY

HABITAT

NOTES

White-winged Scoter *Melanitta fusca*

DATE

LOCALITY

HABITAT

NOTES

Common Goldeneye   *Bucephala clangula*

DATE

LOCALITY

HABITAT

NOTES

Barrow's Goldeneye   *Bucephala islandica*

DATE

LOCALITY

HABITAT

NOTES

Bufflehead   *Bucephala albeola*

DATE

LOCALITY

HABITAT

NOTES

Smew   *Mergellus albellus*

DATE

LOCALITY

HABITAT

NOTES

Hooded Merganser — *Lophodytes cucullatus*

DATE

LOCALITY

HABITAT

NOTES

Common Merganser — *Mergus merganser*

DATE

LOCALITY

HABITAT

NOTES

Red-breasted Merganser — *Mergus serrator*

DATE

LOCALITY

HABITAT

NOTES

Ruddy Duck — *Oxyura jamaicensis*

DATE

LOCALITY

HABITAT

NOTES

Masked Duck   *Oxyura dominica*

DATE

LOCALITY

HABITAT

NOTES

American Vultures (*Cathartidae*)

Black Vulture   *Coragyps atratus*

DATE

LOCALITY

HABITAT

NOTES

Turkey Vulture   *Cathartes aura*

DATE

LOCALITY

HABITAT

NOTES

California Condor   *Gymnogyps californianus*

DATE

LOCALITY

HABITAT

NOTES

F
A
L
C
O
N
I
F
O
R
M
E
S

Ospreys, Kites, Eagles and Hawks
(*Accipitridae*)

Osprey   *Pandion haliaetus*

DATE

LOCALITY

HABITAT

NOTES

Hook-billed Kite   *Chondrohierax uncinatus*

DATE

LOCALITY

HABITAT

NOTES

American Swallow-tailed Kite   *Elanoides forficatus*

DATE

LOCALITY

HABITAT

NOTES

Black-shouldered Kite   *Elanus caeruleus*

DATE

LOCALITY

HABITAT

NOTES

Snail Kite   *Rostrhamus sociabilis*

DATE

LOCALITY

HABITAT

NOTES

Mississippi Kite   *Ictinia mississippiensis*

DATE

LOCALITY

HABITAT

NOTES

Bald Eagle   *Haliaeetus leucocephalus*

DATE

LOCALITY

HABITAT

NOTES

White-tailed Eagle   *Haliaeetus albicilla*

DATE

LOCALITY

HABITAT

NOTES

Steller's Sea-Eagle   *Haliaeetus pelagicus*

DATE

LOCALITY

HABITAT

NOTES

Northern Harrier   *Circus cyaneus*

DATE

LOCALITY

HABITAT

NOTES

Sharp-shinned Hawk   *Accipiter striatus*

DATE

LOCALITY

HABITAT

NOTES

Cooper's Hawk   *Accipiter cooperii*

DATE

LOCALITY

HABITAT

NOTES

Northern Goshawk *Accipiter gentilis*

DATE

LOCALITY

HABITAT

NOTES

Common Black-Hawk *Buteogallus anthracinus*

DATE

LOCALITY

HABITAT

NOTES

Harris' Hawk *Parabuteo unicinctus*

DATE

LOCALITY

HABITAT

NOTES

Gray Hawk *Buteo nitidus*

DATE

LOCALITY

HABITAT

NOTES

Roadside Hawk   *Buteo magnirostris*

DATE

LOCALITY

HABITAT

NOTES

Red-shouldered Hawk   *Buteo lineatus*

DATE

LOCALITY

HABITAT

NOTES

Broad-winged Hawk   *Buteo platypterus*

DATE

LOCALITY

HABITAT

NOTES

Short-tailed Hawk   *Buteo brachyurus*

DATE

LOCALITY

HABITAT

NOTES

Swainson's Hawk — *Buteo swainsoni*

DATE

LOCALITY

HABITAT

NOTES

White-tailed Hawk — *Buteo albicaudatus*

DATE

LOCALITY

HABITAT

NOTES

Zone-tailed Hawk — *Buteo albonotatus*

DATE

LOCALITY

HABITAT

NOTES

Red-tailed Hawk — *Buteo jamaicensis*

DATE

LOCALITY

HABITAT

NOTES

Ferruginous Hawk   *Buteo regalis*

DATE

LOCALITY

HABITAT

NOTES

Rough-legged Hawk   *Buteo lagopus*

DATE

LOCALITY

HABITAT

NOTES

Golden Eagle   *Aquila chrysaetos*

DATE

LOCALITY

HABITAT

NOTES

Falcons and Caracaras (*Falconidae*)

Crested Caracara   *Polyborus plancus*

DATE

LOCALITY

HABITAT

NOTES

Eurasian Kestrel   *Falco tinnunculus*

DATE

LOCALITY

HABITAT

NOTES

American Kestrel   *Falco sparverius*

DATE

LOCALITY

HABITAT

NOTES

Merlin   *Falco columbarius*

DATE

LOCALITY

HABITAT

NOTES

Aplomado Falcon   *Falco femoralis*

DATE

LOCALITY

HABITAT

NOTES

Peregrine Falcon · *Falco peregrinus*

DATE

LOCALITY

HABITAT

NOTES

Gyrfalcon · *Falco rusticolus*

DATE

LOCALITY

HABITAT

NOTES

Prairie Falcon · *Falco mexicanus*

DATE

LOCALITY

HABITAT

NOTES

Chachalacas (*Cracidae*)

Plain Chachalaca · *Ortalis vetula*

DATE

LOCALITY

HABITAT

NOTES

Partridges, Pheasants, Grouse, Turkeys and Quail (*Phasianidae*)

Gray Partridge   *Perdix perdix*

DATE

LOCALITY

HABITAT

NOTES

Black Francolin   *Francolinus francolinus*

DATE

LOCALITY

HABITAT

NOTES

Chukar   *Alectoris chukar*

DATE

LOCALITY

HABITAT

NOTES

Ring-necked Pheasant   *Phasianus colchicus*

DATE

LOCALITY

HABITAT

NOTES

Spruce Grouse   *Dendragapus canadensis*

DATE

LOCALITY

HABITAT

NOTES

Blue Grouse   *Dendragapus obscurus*

DATE

LOCALITY

HABITAT

NOTES

Willow Ptarmigan   *Lagopus lagopus*

DATE

LOCALITY

HABITAT

NOTES

Rock Ptarmigan   *Lagopus mutus*

DATE

LOCALITY

HABITAT

NOTES

White-tailed Ptarmigan   *Logopus leucurus*

DATE

LOCALITY

HABITAT

NOTES

Ruffed Grouse   *Bonasa umbellus*

DATE

LOCALITY

HABITAT

NOTES

Sage Grouse   *Centrocercus urophasianus*

DATE

LOCALITY

HABITAT

NOTES

Greater Prairie-Chicken   *Tympanuchus cupido*

DATE

LOCALITY

HABITAT

NOTES

Lesser Prairie-Chicken *Tympanuchus pallidicinctus*

DATE

LOCALITY

HABITAT

NOTES

Sharp-tailed Grouse *Tympanuchus phasianellus*

DATE

LOCALITY

HABITAT

NOTES

Wild Turkey *Meleagris gallopavo*

DATE

LOCALITY

HABITAT

NOTES

Montezuma Quail *Cyrtonyx montezumae*

DATE

LOCALITY

HABITAT

NOTES

Northern Bobwhite · *Colinus virginianus*

DATE

LOCALITY

HABITAT

NOTES

Scaled Quail · *Callipepla squamata*

DATE

LOCALITY

HABITAT

NOTES

Gambel's Quail · *Callipepla gambelii*

DATE

LOCALITY

HABITAT

NOTES

California Quail · *Callipepla californica*

DATE

LOCALITY

HABITAT

NOTES

Mountain Quail   *Oreortyx pictus*

DATE

LOCALITY

HABITAT

NOTES

Rails, Gallinules and Coots (*Rallidae*)

Yellow Rail   *Coturnicops noveboracensis*

DATE

LOCALITY

HABITAT

NOTES

Black Rail   *Latterallus jamaicensis*

DATE

LOCALITY

HABITAT

NOTES

Corn Crake   *Crex Crex*

DATE

LOCALITY

HABITAT

NOTES

Clapper Rail   *Rallus longirostris*

DATE

LOCALITY

HABITAT

NOTES

King Rail   *Rallus elegans*

DATE

LOCALITY

HABITAT

NOTES

Virginia Rail   *Rallus limicola*

DATE

LOCALITY

HABITAT

NOTES

Sora   *Porzana carolina*

DATE

LOCALITY

HABITAT

NOTES

Paint-billed Crake   *Neocrex erythrops*

DATE

LOCALITY

HABITAT

NOTES

Spotted Rail   *Pardirallus maculatus*

DATE

LOCALITY

HABITAT

NOTES

Purple Gallinule   *Porphyrula martinica*

DATE

LOCALITY

HABITAT

NOTES

Common Moorhen   *Gallinula chloropus*

DATE

LOCALITY

HABITAT

NOTES

Eurasian Coot   *Fulica atra*

DATE

LOCALITY

HABITAT

NOTES

American Coot   *Fulica americana*

DATE

LOCALITY

HABITAT

NOTES

Caribbean Coot   *Fulica caribaea*

DATE

LOCALITY

HABITAT

NOTES

Limpkins (*Aramidae*)

Limpkin   *Aramus guarauna*

DATE

LOCALITY

HABITAT

NOTES

Cranes (*Gruidae*)

Sandhill Crane   *Grus canadensis*

DATE

LOCALITY

HABITAT

NOTES

Common Crane   *Grus grus*

DATE

LOCALITY

HABITAT

NOTES

Whooping Crane   *Grus americana*

DATE

LOCALITY

HABITAT

NOTES

Thick-Knees (*Burhinidae*)

Double-striped Thick-knee   *Burhinus bistriatus*

DATE

LOCALITY

HABITAT

NOTES

Plovers and Lapwings (*Charadriidae*)

Northern Lapwing — *Vanellus vanellus*

DATE

LOCALITY

HABITAT

NOTES

Black-bellied Plover — *Pluvialis squatarola*

DATE

LOCALITY

HABITAT

NOTES

Greater Golden Plover — *Pluvialis apricaria*

DATE

LOCALITY

HABITAT

NOTES

Lesser Golden Plover — *Pluvialis dominica*

DATE

LOCALITY

HABITAT

NOTES

CHARADRIIFORMES

Mongolian Plover   *Charadrius mongolus*

DATE

LOCALITY

HABITAT

NOTES

Snowy Plover   *Charadrius alexandrinus*

DATE

LOCALITY

HABITAT

NOTES

Wilson's Plover   *Charadrius wilsonia*

DATE

LOCALITY

HABITAT

NOTES

Common Ringed Plover   *Charadrius hiaticula*

DATE

LOCALITY

HABITAT

NOTES

Semipalmated Plover *Charadrius semipalmatus*

DATE

LOCALITY

HABITAT

NOTES

Piping Plover *Charadrius melodus*

DATE

LOCALITY

HABITAT

NOTES

Little Ringed Plover *Charadrius dubius*

DATE

LOCALITY

HABITAT

NOTES

Killdeer *Charadrius vociferus*

DATE

LOCALITY

HABITAT

NOTES

Mountain Plover   *Charadrius montanus*

DATE

LOCALITY

HABITAT

NOTES

Eurasian Dotterel   *Charadrius morinellus*

DATE

LOCALITY

HABITAT

NOTES

Oystercatchers (*Haematopodidae*)

American Oystercatcher   *Haematopus palliatus*

DATE

LOCALITY

HABITAT

NOTES

American Black Oystercatcher
Haematopus bachmani

DATE

LOCALITY

HABITAT

NOTES

Stilts and Avocets *(Recurvirostridae)*

Black-necked Stilt   *Himantopus mexicanus*

DATE

LOCALITY

HABITAT

NOTES

American Avocet   *Recurvirostra americana*

DATE

LOCALITY

HABITAT

NOTES

Jacanas *(Jacanidae)*

Northern Jacana   *Jacana spinosa*

DATE

LOCALITY

HABITAT

NOTES

Sandpipers, Phalaropes and Allies *(Scolopacidae)*

Common Greenshank   *Tringa nebularia*

DATE

LOCALITY

HABITAT

NOTES

Greater Yellowlegs   *Tringa melanoleuca*

DATE

LOCALITY

HABITAT

NOTES

Lesser Yellowlegs   *Tringa flavipes*

DATE

LOCALITY

HABITAT

NOTES

Marsh Sandpiper   *Tringa stagnatilis*

DATE

LOCALITY

HABITAT

NOTES

Spotted Redshank   *Tringa erythropus*

DATE

LOCALITY

HABITAT

NOTES

Wood Sandpiper   *Tringa glareola*

DATE

LOCALITY

HABITAT

NOTES

Solitary Sandpiper   *Tringa solitaria*

DATE

LOCALITY

HABITAT

NOTES

Willet   *Catoptrophorus semipalmatus*

DATE

LOCALITY

HABITAT

NOTES

Wandering Tattler   *Heteroscelus incanus*

DATE

LOCALITY

HABITAT

NOTES

Gray-tailed Tattler   *Heteroscelus brevipes*

DATE

LOCALITY

HABITAT

NOTES

Common Sandpiper   *Actitis hypoleucos*

DATE

LOCALITY

HABITAT

NOTES

Spotted Sandpiper   *Actitis macularia*

DATE

LOCALITY

HABITAT

NOTES

Terek Sandpiper   *Xenus cinereus*

DATE

LOCALITY

HABITAT

NOTES

Upland Sandpiper   *Bartramia longicauda*

DATE

LOCALITY

HABITAT

NOTES

Little Curlew   *Numenius minutus*

DATE

LOCALITY

HABITAT

NOTES

Eskimo Curlew   *Numenius borealis*

DATE

LOCALITY

HABITAT

NOTES

Whimbrel   *Numenius phaeopus*

DATE

LOCALITY

HABITAT

NOTES

Bristle-thighed Curlew   *Numenius tahitiensis*

DATE

LOCALITY

HABITAT

NOTES

Slender-billed Curlew   *Numenius tenuirostris*

DATE

LOCALITY

HABITAT

NOTES

Far Eastern Curlew
Numenius madagascariensis

DATE

LOCALITY

HABITAT

NOTES

Eurasian Curlew   *Numenius arquata*

DATE

LOCALITY

HABITAT

NOTES

Long-billed Curlew *Numenius americanus*

DATE

LOCALITY

HABITAT

NOTES

Black-tailed Godwit *Limosa limosa*

DATE

LOCALITY

HABITAT

NOTES

Hudsonian Godwit *Limosa haemastica*

DATE

LOCALITY

HABITAT

NOTES

Bar-tailed Godwit *Limosa lapponica*

DATE

LOCALITY

HABITAT

NOTES

Marbled Godwit   *Limosa fedoa*

DATE

LOCALITY

HABITAT

NOTES

Ruddy Turnstone   *Arenaria interpres*

DATE

LOCALITY

HABITAT

NOTES

Black Turnstone   *Arenaria melanocephala*

DATE

LOCALITY

HABITAT

NOTES

Surfbird   *Aphriza virgata*

DATE

LOCALITY

HABITAT

NOTES

Red Knot   *Calidris canutus*

DATE

LOCALITY

HABITAT

NOTES

Great Knot   *Calidris tenuirostris*

DATE

LOCALITY

HABITAT

NOTES

Sanderling   *Calidris alba*

DATE

LOCALITY

HABITAT

NOTES

Semipalmated Sandpiper   *Calidris pusilla*

DATE

LOCALITY

HABITAT

NOTES

Western Sandpiper   *Calidris mauri*

DATE

LOCALITY

HABITAT

NOTES

Rufous-necked Stint   *Calidris ruficollis*

DATE

LOCALITY

HABITAT

NOTES

Little Stint   *Calidris minuta*

DATE

LOCALITY

HABITAT

NOTES

Temminck's Stint   *Calidris temminckii*

DATE

LOCALITY

HABITAT

NOTES

Long-toed Stint   *Calidris subminuta*

DATE

LOCALITY

HABITAT

NOTES

Least Sandpiper   *Calidris minutilla*

DATE

LOCALITY

HABITAT

NOTES

White-rumped Sandpiper   *Calidris fuscicollis*

DATE

LOCALITY

HABITAT

NOTES

Baird's Sandpiper   *Calidris bairdii*

DATE

LOCALITY

HABITAT

NOTES

Pectoral Sandpiper   *Calidris melanotos*

DATE

LOCALITY

HABITAT

NOTES

Sharp-tailed Sandpiper   *Calidris acuminata*

DATE

LOCALITY

HABITAT

NOTES

Purple Sandpiper   *Calidris maritima*

DATE

LOCALITY

HABITAT

NOTES

Rock Sandpiper   *Calidris ptilocnemis*

DATE

LOCALITY

HABITAT

NOTES

Dunlin   *Calidris alpina*

DATE

LOCALITY

HABITAT

NOTES

Curlew Sandpiper   *Calidris ferruginea*

DATE

LOCALITY

HABITAT

NOTES

Stilt Sandpiper   *Calidris himantopus*

DATE

LOCALITY

HABITAT

NOTES

Spoonbill Sandpiper   *Eurynorhynchos pygmeus*

DATE

LOCALITY

HABITAT

NOTES

Broad-billed Sandpiper   *Limicola falcinellus*

DATE

LOCALITY

HABITAT

NOTES

Buff-breasted Sandpiper   *Tryngites subruficollis*

DATE

LOCALITY

HABITAT

NOTES

Ruff   *Philomachus pugnax*

DATE

LOCALITY

HABITAT

NOTES

Short-billed Dowitcher   *Limnodromus griseus*

DATE

LOCALITY

HABITAT

NOTES

Long-billed Dowitcher   *Limnodromus scolopaceus*

DATE

LOCALITY

HABITAT

NOTES

Jack Snipe   *Lymnocryptes minimus*

DATE

LOCALITY

HABITAT

NOTES

Common Snipe   *Gallinago gallinago*

DATE

LOCALITY

HABITAT

NOTES

Eurasian Woodcock   *Scolopax rusticola*

DATE

LOCALITY

HABITAT

NOTES

American Woodcock   *Scolopax minor*

DATE

LOCALITY

HABITAT

NOTES

Wilson's Phalarope   *Phalaropus tricolor*

DATE

LOCALITY

HABITAT

NOTES

Red-necked Phalarope   *Phalaropus lobatus*

DATE

LOCALITY

HABITAT

NOTES

Red Phalarope   *Phalaropus fulicaria*

DATE

LOCALITY

HABITAT

NOTES

Skuas, Gulls, Terns, Jaegers and Skimmers (*Laridae*)

Pomarine Jaeger   *Stercorarius pomarinus*

DATE

LOCALITY

HABITAT

NOTES

Parasitic Jaeger   *Stercorarius parasiticus*

DATE

LOCALITY

HABITAT

NOTES

Long-tailed Jaeger   *Stercorarius longicaudus*

DATE

LOCALITY

HABITAT

NOTES

Great Skua   *Catharacta skua*

DATE

LOCALITY

HABITAT

NOTES

South Polar Skua — *Catharacta maccormicki*

DATE

LOCALITY

HABITAT

NOTES

Laughing Gull — *Larus atricilla*

DATE

LOCALITY

HABITAT

NOTES

Franklin's Gull — *Larus pipixcan*

DATE

LOCALITY

HABITAT

NOTES

Little Gull — *Larus minutus*

DATE

LOCALITY

HABITAT

NOTES

Common Black-headed Gull   *Larus ridibundus*

DATE

LOCALITY

HABITAT

NOTES

Bonaparte's Gull   *Larus philadephia*

DATE

LOCALITY

HABITAT

NOTES

Heermann's Gull   *Larus heermanni*

DATE

LOCALITY

HABITAT

NOTES

Mew Gull   *Larus canus*

DATE

LOCALITY

HABITAT

NOTES

Ring-billed Gull   *Larus delawarensis*

DATE

LOCALITY

HABITAT

NOTES

California Gull   *Larus californicus*

DATE

LOCALITY

HABITAT

NOTES

Herring Gull   *Larus argentatus*

DATE

LOCALITY

HABITAT

NOTES

Thayer's Gull   *Larus thayeri*

DATE

LOCALITY

HABITAT

NOTES

Iceland Gull   *Larus glaucoides*

DATE

LOCALITY

HABITAT

NOTES

Lesser Black-backed Gull   *Larus fuscus*

DATE

LOCALITY

HABITAT

NOTES

Slaty-backed Gull   *Larus schistisagus*

DATE

LOCALITY

HABITAT

NOTES

Yellow-footed Gull   *Larus livens*

DATE

LOCALITY

HABITAT

NOTES

Western Gull   *Larus occidentalis*

DATE

LOCALITY

HABITAT

NOTES

Glaucous-winged Gull   *Larus glaucescens*

DATE

LOCALITY

HABITAT

NOTES

Glaucous Gull   *Larus hyperboreus*

DATE

LOCALITY

HABITAT

NOTES

Great Black-backed Gull   *Larus marinus*

DATE

LOCALITY

HABITAT

NOTES

Black-legged Kittiwake · *Rissa tridactyla*

DATE

LOCALITY

HABITAT

NOTES

Red-legged Kittiwake · *Rissa brevirostris*

DATE

LOCALITY

HABITAT

NOTES

Ross' Gull · *Rhodostethia rosea*

DATE

LOCALITY

HABITAT

NOTES

Sabine's Gull · *Xema sabini*

DATE

LOCALITY

HABITAT

NOTES

Ivory Gull   *Pagophila eburnea*

DATE

LOCALITY

HABITAT

NOTES

Gull-billed Tern   *Sterna nilotica*

DATE

LOCALITY

HABITAT

NOTES

Caspian Tern   *Sterna caspia*

DATE

LOCALITY

HABITAT

NOTES

Royal Tern   *Sterna maxima*

DATE

LOCALITY

HABITAT

NOTES

Elegant Tern   *Sterna elegans*

DATE

LOCALITY

HABITAT

NOTES

Sandwich Tern   *Sterna sandvicensis*

DATE

LOCALITY

HABITAT

NOTES

Roseate Tern   *Sterna dougallii*

DATE

LOCALITY

HABITAT

NOTES

Common Tern   *Sterna hirundo*

DATE

LOCALITY

HABITAT

NOTES

Arctic Tern   *Sterna paradisaea*

DATE

LOCALITY

HABITAT

NOTES

Forster's Tern   *Sterna forsteri*

DATE

LOCALITY

HABITAT

NOTES

Least Tern   *Sterna antillarum*

DATE

LOCALITY

HABITAT

NOTES

Aleutian Tern   *Sterna aleutica*

DATE

LOCALITY

HABITAT

NOTES

Bridled Tern
Sterna anaethetus

DATE

LOCALITY

HABITAT

NOTES

Sooty Tern
Sterna fuscata

DATE

LOCALITY

HABITAT

NOTES

White-winged Tern
Chlidonias leucopterus

DATE

LOCALITY

HABITAT

NOTES

Black Tern
Chlidonias niger

DATE

LOCALITY

HABITAT

NOTES

Brown Noddy *Anous stolidus*

DATE

LOCALITY

HABITAT

NOTES

Black Noddy *Anous minutus*

DATE

LOCALITY

HABITAT

NOTES

Black Skimmer *Rynchops niger*

DATE

LOCALITY

HABITAT

NOTES

Auks, Murres and Puffins (*Alcidae*)

Dovekie *Alle alle*

DATE

LOCALITY

HABITAT

NOTES

Common Murre   *Uria aalge*

DATE

LOCALITY

HABITAT

NOTES

Thick-billed Murre   *Uria lomvia*

DATE

LOCALITY

HABITAT

NOTES

Razorbill   *Alca torda*

DATE

LOCALITY

HABITAT

NOTES

Black Guillemot   *Cepphus grylle*

DATE

LOCALITY

HABITAT

NOTES

Pigeon Guillemot   *Cepphus columba*

DATE

LOCALITY

HABITAT

NOTES

Marbled Murrelet   *Brachyramphus marmoratus*

DATE

LOCALITY

HABITAT

NOTES

Kittlitz's Murrelet   *Brachyramphus brevirostris*

DATE

LOCALITY

HABITAT

NOTES

Xantus' Murrelet   *Synthliboramphus hypoleucus*

DATE

LOCALITY

HABITAT

NOTES

Craveri's Murrelet   *Synthliboramphus craveri*

DATE

LOCALITY

HABITAT

NOTES

Ancient Murrelet   *Synthliboramphus antiquus*

DATE

LOCALITY

HABITAT

NOTES

Cassin's Auklet   *Ptychoramphys aleuticus*

DATE

LOCALITY

HABITAT

NOTES

Parakeet Auklet   *Cyclorrhynchus psittacula*

DATE

LOCALITY

HABITAT

NOTES

Least Auklet   *Aethia pusilla*

DATE

LOCALITY

HABITAT

NOTES

Whiskered Auklet   *Aethia pygmaea*

DATE

LOCALITY

HABITAT

NOTES

Crested Auklet   *Aethia cristatella*

DATE

LOCALITY

HABITAT

NOTES

Rhinoceros Auklet   *Cerorhinca monocerata*

DATE

LOCALITY

HABITAT

NOTES

Tufted Puffin   *Fratercula cirrhata*

DATE

LOCALITY

HABITAT

NOTES

Atlantic Puffin   *Fratercula arctica*

DATE

LOCALITY

HABITAT

NOTES

Horned Puffin   *Fratercula corniculata*

DATE

LOCALITY

HABITAT

NOTES

Pigeons and Doves (*Columbidae*)

Rock Dove   *Columba livia*

DATE

LOCALITY

HABITAT

NOTES

C
O
L
U
M
B
I
F
O
R
M
E
S

Scaly-naped Pigeon   *Columba squamosa*

DATE

LOCALITY

HABITAT

NOTES

White-crowned Pigeon   *Columba leucocephala*

DATE

LOCALITY

HABITAT

NOTES

Red-billed Pigeon   *Columba flavirostris*

DATE

LOCALITY

HABITAT

NOTES

Band-tailed Pigeon   *Columba fasciata*

DATE

LOCALITY

HABITAT

NOTES

Ringed Turtle-Dove — *Streptopelia risoria*

DATE

LOCALITY

HABITAT

NOTES

Spotted Dove — *Streptopelia chinensis*

DATE

LOCALITY

HABITAT

NOTES

White-winged Dove — *Zenaida asiatica*

DATE

LOCALITY

HABITAT

NOTES

Zenaida Dove — *Zenaida aurita*

DATE

LOCALITY

HABITAT

NOTES

Mourning Dove   *Zenaida macroura*

DATE

LOCALITY

HABITAT

NOTES

Inca Dove   *Columbina inca*

DATE

LOCALITY

HABITAT

NOTES

Common Ground-Dove   *Columbina passerina*

DATE

LOCALITY

HABITAT

NOTES

Ruddy Ground-Dove   *Columbina talpacoti*

DATE

LOCALITY

HABITAT

NOTES

White-tipped Dove   *Leptotila verreauxi*

DATE

LOCALITY

HABITAT

NOTES

Key West Quail-Dove   *Geotrygon chrysia*

DATE

LOCALITY

HABITAT

NOTES

Ruddy Quail-Dove   *Geotrygon montana*

DATE

LOCALITY

HABITAT

NOTES

Parakeets and Parrots *(Psittacidae)*

Budgerigar   *Melopsittacus undulatus*

DATE

LOCALITY

HABITAT

NOTES

P
S
I
T
T
A
C
I
F
O
R
M
E
S

Rose-ringed Parakeet   *Psittacula krameri*

DATE

LOCALITY

HABITAT

NOTES

Monk Parakeet   *Myopsitta monachus*

DATE

LOCALITY

HABITAT

NOTES

Thick-billed Parrot
Rhynchopsitta pachyrhyncha

DATE

LOCALITY

HABITAT

NOTES

Canary-winged Parakeet   *Brotogeris versicolurus*

DATE

LOCALITY

HABITAT

NOTES

Red-crowned Parrot *Amazona viridigenalis*

DATE

LOCALITY

HABITAT

NOTES

Yellow-headed Parrot *Amazona oratrix*

DATE

LOCALITY

HABITAT

NOTES

Cuckoos, Roadrunners and Anis (*Cuculidae*)

Common Cuckoo *Cuculus canorus*

DATE

LOCALITY

HABITAT

NOTES

Oriental Cuckoo *Cuculus saturatus*

DATE

LOCALITY

HABITAT

NOTES

CUCULIFORMES

Black-billed Cuckoo   *Coccyzus erythropthalmus*

DATE

LOCALITY

HABITAT

NOTES

Yellow-billed Cuckoo   *Coccyzus americanus*

DATE

LOCALITY

HABITAT

NOTES

Mangrove Cuckoo   *Coccyzus minor*

DATE

LOCALITY

HABITAT

NOTES

Greater Roadrunner   *Geococcyx californianus*

DATE

LOCALITY

HABITAT

NOTES

Smooth-billed Ani   *Crotophaga ani*

DATE

LOCALITY

HABITAT

NOTES

Groove-billed Ani   *Crotophaga sulcirostris*

DATE

LOCALITY

HABITAT

NOTES

Barn Owls *(Tytonidae)*

Common Barn-Owl   *Tyto alba*

DATE

LOCALITY

HABITAT

NOTES

Typical Owls *(Strigidae)*

Oriental Scops-Owl   *Otus sunia*

DATE

LOCALITY

HABITAT

NOTES

S
T
R
I
G
I
F
O
R
M
E
S

Flammulated Owl · *Otus flammeolus*

DATE

LOCALITY

HABITAT

NOTES

Eastern Screech-Owl · *Otus asio*

DATE

LOCALITY

HABITAT

NOTES

Western Screech-Owl · *Otus kennicottii*

DATE

LOCALITY

HABITAT

NOTES

Whiskered Screech-Owl · *Otus trichopsis*

DATE

LOCALITY

HABITAT

NOTES

Great Horned Owl   *Bubo virginianus*

DATE

LOCALITY

HABITAT

NOTES

Snowy Owl   *Nyctea scandiaca*

DATE

LOCALITY

HABITAT

NOTES

Northern Hawk-Owl   *Surnia ulula*

DATE

LOCALITY

HABITAT

NOTES

Northern Pygmy-Owl   *Glaucidium gnoma*

DATE

LOCALITY

HABITAT

NOTES

Ferruginous Pygmy-Owl
Glaucidium brasilianum

DATE

LOCALITY

HABITAT

NOTES

Elf Owl
Micrathene whitneyi

DATE

LOCALITY

HABITAT

NOTES

Burrowing Owl
Athene cunicularia

DATE

LOCALITY

HABITAT

NOTES

Spotted Owl
Strix occidentalis

DATE

LOCALITY

HABITAT

NOTES

Barred Owl *Strix varia*

DATE

LOCALITY

HABITAT

NOTES

Great Gray Owl *Strix nebulosa*

DATE

LOCALITY

HABITAT

NOTES

Long-eared Owl *Asio otus*

DATE

LOCALITY

HABITAT

NOTES

Short-eared Owl *Asio flammeus*

DATE

LOCALITY

HABITAT

NOTES

Boreal Owl · *Aegolius funereus*

DATE

LOCALITY

HABITAT

NOTES

Northern Saw-whet Owl · *Aegolius acadicus*

DATE

LOCALITY

HABITAT

NOTES

Goatsuckers (*Caprimulgidae*)

Lesser Nighthawk · *Chordeiles acutipennis*

DATE

LOCALITY

HABITAT

NOTES

Common Nighthawk · *Chordeiles minor*

DATE

LOCALITY

HABITAT

NOTES

CAPRIMULGIFORMES

Antillean Nighthawk   *Chordeiles gundlachii*

DATE

LOCALITY

HABITAT

NOTES

Common Pauraque   *Nyctidromus albicollis*

DATE

LOCALITY

HABITAT

NOTES

Common Poorwill   *Phalaenoptilus nuttallii*

DATE

LOCALITY

HABITAT

NOTES

Chuck-will's-widow   *Caprimulgus carolinensis*

DATE

LOCALITY

HABITAT

NOTES

Buff-collared Nightjar   *Caprimulgus ridgwayi*

DATE

LOCALITY

HABITAT

NOTES

Whip-poor-will   *Caprimulgus vociferus*

DATE

LOCALITY

HABITAT

NOTES

Jungle Nightjar   *Caprimulgus indicus*

DATE

LOCALITY

HABITAT

NOTES

Swifts (*Apodidae*)

Black Swift   *Cypseloides niger*

DATE

LOCALITY

HABITAT

NOTES

A
P
O
D
I
F
O
R
M
E
S

White-collared Swift   *Streptoprocne zonaris*

DATE

LOCALITY

HABITAT

NOTES

Chimney Swift   *Chaetura pelagica*

DATE

LOCALITY

HABITAT

NOTES

Vaux's Swift   *Chaetura vauxi*

DATE

LOCALITY

HABITAT

NOTES

White-throated Needletail

Hirundapus caudacutus

DATE

LOCALITY

HABITAT

NOTES

Common Swift   *Apus apus*

DATE

LOCALITY

HABITAT

NOTES

Fork-tailed Swift   *Apus pacificus*

DATE

LOCALITY

HABITAT

NOTES

White-throated Swift   *Aeronautes saxatalis*

DATE

LOCALITY

HABITAT

NOTES

Antillean Palm Swift   *Tachornis phoenicobia*

DATE

LOCALITY

HABITAT

NOTES

Hummingbirds (*Trochilidae*)

Green Violet-ear   *Colibri thalassinus*

DATE

LOCALITY

HABITAT

NOTES

Cuban Emerald   *Chlorostilbon ricordii*

DATE

LOCALITY

HABITAT

NOTES

Broad-billed Hummingbird
Cynanthus latirostris

DATE

LOCALITY

HABITAT

NOTES

White-eared Hummingbird   *Hylocharis leucotis*

DATE

LOCALITY

HABITAT

NOTES

Berylline Hummingbird   *Amazilia beryllina*

DATE
....
LOCALITY
....
HABITAT
....
NOTES
....

Rufous-tailed Hummingbird   *Amazilia tzacatl*

DATE
....
LOCALITY
....
HABITAT
....
NOTES
....

Buff-bellied Hummingbird

Amazilia yucatanensis

DATE
....
LOCALITY
....
HABITAT
....
NOTES
....

Violet-crowned Hummingbird

Amazilia violiceps

DATE
....
LOCALITY
....
HABITAT
....
NOTES
....

Blue-throated Hummingbird
Lampornis clemenciae

DATE

LOCALITY

HABITAT

NOTES

Magnificent Hummingbird   *Eugenes fulgens*

DATE

LOCALITY

HABITAT

NOTES

Plain-capped Starthroat   *Heliomaster constantii*

DATE

LOCALITY

HABITAT

NOTES

Bahama Woodstar   *Calliphlox evelynae*

DATE

LOCALITY

HABITAT

NOTES

Lucifer Hummingbird   *Calothorax lucifer*

DATE

LOCALITY

HABITAT

NOTES

Ruby-throated Hummingbird
Archilochus colubris

DATE

LOCALITY

HABITAT

NOTES

Black-chinned Hummingbird
Archilochus alexandri

DATE

LOCALITY

HABITAT

NOTES

Anna's Hummingbird   *Calypte anna*

DATE

LOCALITY

HABITAT

NOTES

Costa's Hummingbird   *Calypte costae*

DATE

LOCALITY

HABITAT

NOTES

Calliope Hummingbird   *Stellula calliope*

DATE

LOCALITY

HABITAT

NOTES

Bumblebee Hummingbird   *Atthis heloisa*

DATE

LOCALITY

HABITAT

NOTES

Broad-tailed Hummingbird

Selasphorus platycercus

DATE

LOCALITY

HABITAT

NOTES

Rufous Hummingbird   *Selasphorus rufus*

DATE

LOCALITY

HABITAT

NOTES

Allen's Hummingbird   *Selasphorus sasin*

DATE

LOCALITY

HABITAT

NOTES

Trogons (*Trogonidae*)

Elegant Trogon   *Trogon elegans*

DATE

LOCALITY

HABITAT

NOTES

Eared Trogon   *Euptilotus neoxenus*

DATE

LOCALITY

HABITAT

NOTES

T
R
O
G
O
N
I
F
O
R
M
E
S

Hoopoes (*Upupidae*)

Hoopoe   *Upupa epops*

DATE

LOCALITY

HABITAT

NOTES

Kingfishers (*Alcedinidae*)

Ringed Kingfisher   *Ceryle torquata*

DATE

LOCALITY

HABITAT

NOTES

Belted Kingfisher   *Ceryle alcyon*

DATE

LOCALITY

HABITAT

NOTES

Green Kingfisher   *Chloroceryle americana*

DATE

LOCALITY

HABITAT

NOTES

CORACIIFORMES

Woodpeckers and Allies *(Picidae)*

Eurasian Wryneck   *Jynx torquilla*

DATE

LOCALITY

HABITAT

NOTES

Lewis' Woodpecker   *Melanerpes lewis*

DATE

LOCALITY

HABITAT

NOTES

Red-headed Woodpecker
Melanerpes erythrocephalus

DATE

LOCALITY

HABITAT

NOTES

Acorn Woodpecker   *Melanerpes formicivorus*

DATE

LOCALITY

HABITAT

NOTES

Gila Woodpecker *Melanerpes uropygialis*

DATE

LOCALITY

HABITAT

NOTES

Golden-fronted Woodpecker
Melanerpes aurifrons

DATE

LOCALITY

HABITAT

NOTES

Red-bellied Woodpecker *Melanerpes carolinus*

DATE

LOCALITY

HABITAT

NOTES

Yellow-bellied Sapsucker *Sphyrapicus varius*

DATE

LOCALITY

HABITAT

NOTES

Red-breasted Sapsucker   *Sphyrapicus ruber*

DATE

LOCALITY

HABITAT

NOTES

Williamson's Sapsucker   *Sphyrapicus thyroideus*

DATE

LOCALITY

HABITAT

NOTES

Ladder-backed Woodpecker   *Picoides scalaris*

DATE

LOCALITY

HABITAT

NOTES

Nuttall's Woodpecker   *Picoides nuttallii*

DATE

LOCALITY

HABITAT

NOTES

Downy Woodpecker *Picoides pubescens*

DATE

LOCALITY

HABITAT

NOTES

Hairy Woodpecker *Picoides villosus*

DATE

LOCALITY

HABITAT

NOTES

Strickland's Woodpecker *Picoides stricklandi*

DATE

LOCALITY

HABITAT

NOTES

Red-cockaded Woodpecker *Picoides borealis*

DATE

LOCALITY

HABITAT

NOTES

White-headed Woodpecker   *Picoides albolarvatus*

DATE

LOCALITY

HABITAT

NOTES

Three-toed Woodpecker   *Picoides tridactylus*

DATE

LOCALITY

HABITAT

NOTES

Black-backed Woodpecker   *Picoides arcticus*

DATE

LOCALITY

HABITAT

NOTES

Northern Flicker   *Colaptes auratus*

DATE

LOCALITY

HABITAT

NOTES

Pileated Woodpecker *Dryocopus pileatus*

DATE

LOCALITY

HABITAT

NOTES

Ivory-billed Woodpecker *Campephilus principalis*

DATE

LOCALITY

HABITAT

NOTES

Tyrant Flycatchers *(Tyrannidae)*

Northern Beardless-Tyrannulet
Camptostoma imberbe

DATE

LOCALITY

HABITAT

NOTES

Olive-sided Flycatcher *Contopus borealisd*

DATE

LOCALITY

HABITAT

NOTES

PASSERIFORMES

Greater Pewee   *Contopus pertinax*

DATE

LOCALITY

HABITAT

NOTES

Western Wood-Pewee   *Contopus sordidulus*

DATE

LOCALITY

HABITAT

NOTES

Eastern Wood-Pewee   *Contopus virens*

DATE

LOCALITY

HABITAT

NOTES

Yellow-bellied Flycatcher   *Empidonax flaviventris*

DATE

LOCALITY

HABITAT

NOTES

Acadian Flycatcher · *Empidonax virescens*

DATE

LOCALITY

HABITAT

NOTES

Alder Flycatcher · *Empidonax alnorum*

DATE

LOCALITY

HABITAT

NOTES

Willow Flycatcher · *Empidonax traillii*

DATE

LOCALITY

HABITAT

NOTES

Least Flycatcher · *Empidonax minimus*

DATE

LOCALITY

HABITAT

NOTES

Hammond's Flycatcher   *Empidonax hammondii*

DATE

LOCALITY

HABITAT

NOTES

Dusky Flycatcher   *Empidonax oberholseri*

DATE

LOCALITY

HABITAT

NOTES

Gray Flycatcher   *Empidonax wrightii*

DATE

LOCALITY

HABITAT

NOTES

Western Flycatcher   *Empidonax difficilis*

DATE

LOCALITY

HABITAT

NOTES

Buff-breasted Flycatcher   *Empidonax fulvifrons*

DATE

LOCALITY

HABITAT

NOTES

Black Phoebe   *Sayornis nigricans*

DATE

LOCALITY

HABITAT

NOTES

Eastern Phoebe   *Sayornis phoebe*

DATE

LOCALITY

HABITAT

NOTES

Say's Phoebe   *Sayornis saya*

DATE

LOCALITY

HABITAT

NOTES

Vermilion Flycatcher   *Pyrocephalus rubinus*

DATE

LOCALITY

HABITAT

NOTES

Dusky-capped Flycatcher   *Myiarchus tuberculifer*

DATE

LOCALITY

HABITAT

NOTES

Ash-throated Flycatcher   *Myiarchus cinerascens*

DATE

LOCALITY

HABITAT

NOTES

Great Crested Flycatcher   *Myiarchus crinitus*

DATE

LOCALITY

HABITAT

NOTES

Brown-crested Flycatcher *Myiarchus tyrannulus*

DATE

LOCALITY

HABITAT

NOTES

Great Kiskadee *Pitangus sulphuratus*

DATE

LOCALITY

HABITAT

NOTES

La Sagra's Flycatcher *Myiarchus sagrae*

DATE

LOCALITY

HABITAT

NOTES

Sulphur-bellied Flycatcher
Myiodynastes luteiventris

DATE

LOCALITY

HABITAT

NOTES

Variegated Flycatcher   *Empidonomus varius*

DATE

LOCALITY

HABITAT

NOTES

Tropical Kingbird   *Tyrannus melancholicus*

DATE

LOCALITY

HABITAT

NOTES

Couch's Kingbird   *Tyrannus couchii*

DATE

LOCALITY

HABITAT

NOTES

Cassin's Kingbird   *Tyrannus vociferans*

DATE

LOCALITY

HABITAT

NOTES

Thick-billed Kingbird   *Tyrannus crassirostris*

DATE

LOCALITY

HABITAT

NOTES

Western Kingbird   *Tyrannus verticalis*

DATE

LOCALITY

HABITAT

NOTES

Eastern Kingbird   *Tyrannus tyrannus*

DATE

LOCALITY

HABITAT

NOTES

Gray Kingbird   *Tyrannus dominicensis*

DATE

LOCALITY

HABITAT

NOTES

Loggerhead Kingbird   *Tyrannus caudifasciatus*

DATE

LOCALITY

HABITAT

NOTES

Scissor-tailed Flycatcher   *Tyrannus forficatus*

DATE

LOCALITY

HABITAT

NOTES

Fork-tailed Flycatcher   *Tyrannus savana*

DATE

LOCALITY

HABITAT

NOTES

Rose-throated Becard   *Pachyramphus aglaiae*

DATE

LOCALITY

HABITAT

NOTES

Larks (*Alaudidae*)

Eurasian Skylark   *Alauda arvensis*

DATE

LOCALITY

HABITAT

NOTES

Horned Lark   *Eremophila alpestris*

DATE

LOCALITY

HABITAT

NOTES

Swallows (*Hirundinidae*)

Purple Martin   *Progne subis*

DATE

LOCALITY

HABITAT

NOTES

Cuban Martin   *Progne cryptoleuca*

DATE

LOCALITY

HABITAT

NOTES

Gray-breasted Martin   *Progne chalybea*

DATE

LOCALITY

HABITAT

NOTES

Southern Martin   *Progne elegans*

DATE

LOCALITY

HABITAT

NOTES

Tree Swallow   *Tachycineta bicolor*

DATE

LOCALITY

HABITAT

NOTES

Violet-green Swallow   *Tachycineta thalassina*

DATE

LOCALITY

HABITAT

NOTES

Bahama Swallow   *Tachycineta cyaneoviridis*

DATE

LOCALITY

HABITAT

NOTES

Northern Rough-winged Swallow
Stelgidopteryx serripennis

DATE

LOCALITY

HABITAT

NOTES

Bank Swallow   *Riparia riparia*

DATE

LOCALITY

HABITAT

NOTES

Cliff Swallow   *Hirundo pyrrhonota*

DATE

LOCALITY

HABITAT

NOTES

Cave Swallow   *Hirundo fulva*

DATE

LOCALITY

HABITAT

NOTES

Barn Swallow   *Hirundo rustica*

DATE

LOCALITY

HABITAT

NOTES

Common House-Martin   *Delichon urbica*

DATE

LOCALITY

HABITAT

NOTES

Jays, Magpies and Crows (*Corvidae*)

Gray Jay   *Perisoreus canadensis*

DATE

LOCALITY

HABITAT

NOTES

Stellar's Jay   *Cyanocitta stelleri*

DATE

LOCALITY

HABITAT

NOTES

Blue Jay   *Cyanocitta cristata*

DATE

LOCALITY

HABITAT

NOTES

Green Jay   *Cyanocorax yncas*

DATE

LOCALITY

HABITAT

NOTES

Brown Jay   *Cyanocorax morio*

DATE

LOCALITY

HABITAT

NOTES

Scrub Jay — *Aphelocoma coerulescens*

DATE

LOCALITY

HABITAT

NOTES

Gray-breasted Jay — *Aphelocoma ultramarina*

DATE

LOCALITY

HABITAT

NOTES

Pinyon Jay — *Gymnorhinus cyanocephalus*

DATE

LOCALITY

HABITAT

NOTES

Clark's Nutcracker — *Nucifraga columbiana*

DATE

LOCALITY

HABITAT

NOTES

Black-billed Magpie   *Pica pica*

DATE

LOCALITY

HABITAT

NOTES

Yellow-billed Magpie   *Pica nuttalli*

DATE

LOCALITY

HABITAT

NOTES

American Crow   *Corvus brachyrhynchos*

DATE

LOCALITY

HABITAT

NOTES

Northwestern Crow   *Corvus caurinus*

DATE

LOCALITY

HABITAT

NOTES

Mexican Crow   *Corvus imparatus*

DATE

LOCALITY

HABITAT

NOTES

Fish Crow   *Corvus ossifragus*

DATE

LOCALITY

HABITAT

NOTES

Chihuahuan Raven   *Corvus cryptoleucus*

DATE

LOCALITY

HABITAT

NOTES

Common Raven   *Corvus corax*

DATE

LOCALITY

HABITAT

NOTES

Titmice (*Paridae*)

Black-capped Chickadee   *Parus atricapillus*

DATE

LOCALITY

HABITAT

NOTES

Carolina Chickadee   *Parus carolinensis*

DATE

LOCALITY

HABITAT

NOTES

Mexican Chickadee   *Parus sclateri*

DATE

LOCALITY

HABITAT

NOTES

Mountain Chickadee   *Parus gambeli*

DATE

LOCALITY

HABITAT

NOTES

Siberian Tit   *Parus cinctus*

DATE

LOCALITY

HABITAT

NOTES

Boreal Chickadee   *Parus hudsonicus*

DATE

LOCALITY

HABITAT

NOTES

Chestnut-backed Chickadee   *Parus rufescens*

DATE

LOCALITY

HABITAT

NOTES

Bridled Titmouse   *Parus wollweberi*

DATE

LOCALITY

HABITAT

NOTES

Plain Titmouse — *Parus inornatus*

DATE

LOCALITY

HABITAT

NOTES

Tufted Titmouse — *Parus bicolor*

DATE

LOCALITY

HABITAT

NOTES

Verdins (*Remizidae*)

Verdin — *Auriparus flaviceps*

DATE

LOCALITY

HABITAT

NOTES

Bushtits (*Aegithalidae*)

Bushtit — *Psaltriparus minimus*

DATE

LOCALITY

HABITAT

NOTES

Nuthatches *(Sittidae)*

Red-breasted Nuthatch   *Sitta canadensis*

DATE

LOCALITY

HABITAT

NOTES

White-breasted Nuthatch   *Sitta carolinensis*

DATE

LOCALITY

HABITAT

NOTES

Pygmy Nuthatch   *Sitta pygmaea*

DATE

LOCALITY

HABITAT

NOTES

Brown-headed Nuthatch   *Sitta pusilla*

DATE

LOCALITY

HABITAT

NOTES

Creepers (*Certhiidae*)

Brown Creeper   *Certhia americana*

DATE

LOCALITY

HABITAT

NOTES

Bulbuls (*Pycnonotidae*)

Red-whiskered Bulbul   *Pycnonotus jocosus*

DATE

LOCALITY

HABITAT

NOTES

Wrens (*Troglodytidae*)

Cactus Wren   *Campylorhynchus brunneicapillus*

DATE

LOCALITY

HABITAT

NOTES

Rock Wren   *Salpinctes obsoletus*

DATE

LOCALITY

HABITAT

NOTES

Canyon Wren   *Catherpes mexicanus*

DATE

LOCALITY

HABITAT

NOTES

Carolina Wren   *Thryothorus ludovicianus*

DATE

LOCALITY

HABITAT

NOTES

Bewick's Wren   *Thryomanes bewickii*

DATE

LOCALITY

HABITAT

NOTES

House Wren   *Troglodytes aedon*

DATE

LOCALITY

HABITAT

NOTES

Winter Wren   *Troglodytes troglodytes*

DATE

LOCALITY

HABITAT

NOTES

Sedge Wren   *Cistothorus platensis*

DATE

LOCALITY

HABITAT

NOTES

Marsh Wren   *Cistothorus palustris*

DATE

LOCALITY

HABITAT

NOTES

Dippers *(Muscicapidae)*

American Dipper   *Cinclus mexicanus*

DATE

LOCALITY

HABITAT

NOTES

Old World Warblers, Kinglets and Gnatcatchers; Old World Flycatchers and Allies; Solitaires, Thrushes and Allies (*Muscicapidae*)

Middendorf's Grasshopper Warbler
Locustella ochotensis

DATE

LOCALITY

HABITAT

NOTES

Wood Warbler   *Phylloscopus sibilatrix*

DATE

LOCALITY

HABITAT

NOTES

Dusky Warbler   *Phylloscopus fuscatus*

DATE

LOCALITY

HABITAT

NOTES

Arctic Warbler   *Phylloscopus borealis*

DATE

LOCALITY

HABITAT

NOTES

Golden-crowned Kinglet   *Regulus satrapa*

DATE

LOCALITY

HABITAT

NOTES

Ruby-crowned Kinglet   *Regulus calendula*

DATE

LOCALITY

HABITAT

NOTES

Blue-gray Gnatcatcher   *Polioptila caerulea*

DATE

LOCALITY

HABITAT

NOTES

Black-tailed Gnatcatcher   *Polioptila melanura*

DATE

LOCALITY

HABITAT

NOTES

Black-capped Gnatcatcher   *Polioptila nigriceps*

DATE

LOCALITY

HABITAT

NOTES

Red-breasted Flycatcher   *Ficedula parva*

DATE

LOCALITY

HABITAT

NOTES

Siberian Flycatcher   *Muscicapa sibirica*

DATE

LOCALITY

HABITAT

NOTES

Gray-spotted Flycatcher   *Muscicapa griseisticta*

DATE

LOCALITY

HABITAT

NOTES

Siberian Rubythroat   *Luscinia calliope*

DATE

LOCALITY

HABITAT

NOTES

Bluethroat   *Luscinia svecica*

DATE

LOCALITY

HABITAT

NOTES

Northern Wheatear   *Oenanthe oenanthe*

DATE

LOCALITY

HABITAT

NOTES

Eastern Bluebird   *Sialia sialis*

DATE

LOCALITY

HABITAT

NOTES

Western Bluebird   *Sialia mexicana*

DATE

LOCALITY

HABITAT

NOTES

Mountain Bluebird   *Sialia currucoides*

DATE

LOCALITY

HABITAT

NOTES

Townsend's Solitaire   *Myadestes townsendi*

DATE

LOCALITY

HABITAT

NOTES

Veery   *Catharus fuscescens*

DATE

LOCALITY

HABITAT

NOTES

Gray-cheeked Thrush   *Catharus minimus*

DATE

LOCALITY

HABITAT

NOTES

Swainson's Thrush   *Catharus ustulatus*

DATE

LOCALITY

HABITAT

NOTES

Hermit Thrush   *Catharus guttatus*

DATE

LOCALITY

HABITAT

NOTES

Wood Thrush   *Hylocichla mustelina*

DATE

LOCALITY

HABITAT

NOTES

Eye-browed Thrush   *Turdus obscurus*

DATE

LOCALITY

HABITAT

NOTES

Dusky Thrush   *Turdus naumanni*

DATE

LOCALITY

HABITAT

NOTES

Fieldfare   *Turdus pilaris*

DATE

LOCALITY

HABITAT

NOTES

Clay-colored Robin   *Turdus grayi*

DATE

LOCALITY

HABITAT

NOTES

Rufous-backed Robin　　　　*Turdus rufopalliatus*

DATE

LOCALITY

HABITAT

NOTES

American Robin　　　　*Turdus migratorius*

DATE

LOCALITY

HABITAT

NOTES

Varied Thrush　　　　*Ixoreus naevius*

DATE

LOCALITY

HABITAT

NOTES

Aztec Thrush　　　　*Ridgwayia pinicola*

DATE

LOCALITY

HABITAT

NOTES

Wrentit   *Chamaea fasciata*

DATE

LOCALITY

HABITAT

NOTES

Mockingbirds, Thrashers and Allies (*Mimidae*)

Gray Catbird   *Dumetella carolinensis*

DATE

LOCALITY

HABITAT

NOTES

Northern Mockingbird   *Mimus polyglottos*

DATE

LOCALITY

HABITAT

NOTES

Bahama Mockingbird   *Mimus gundlachii*

DATE

LOCALITY

HABITAT

NOTES

Sage Thrasher — *Oreoscoptes montanus*

DATE

LOCALITY

HABITAT

NOTES

Brown Thrasher — *Toxostoma rufum*

DATE

LOCALITY

HABITAT

NOTES

Long-billed Thrasher — *Toxostoma longirostre*

DATE

LOCALITY

HABITAT

NOTES

Bendire's Thrasher — *Toxostoma bendirei*

DATE

LOCALITY

HABITAT

NOTES

Curve-billed Thrasher   *Toxostoma curvirostre*

DATE

LOCALITY

HABITAT

NOTES

California Thrasher   *Toxostoma redivivum*

DATE

LOCALITY

HABITAT

NOTES

Crissal Thrasher   *Toxostoma dorsale*

DATE

LOCALITY

HABITAT

NOTES

Le Conte's Thrasher   *Toxostoma lecontei*

DATE

LOCALITY

HABITAT

NOTES

Accentors (*Prunellidae*)

Siberian Accentor   *Prunella montanella*

DATE

LOCALITY

HABITAT

NOTES

Wagtails and Pipits (*Motacillidae*)

Yellow Wagtail   *Motacilla flava*

DATE

LOCALITY

HABITAT

NOTES

Gray Wagtail   *Motacilla cinerea*

DATE

LOCALITY

HABITAT

NOTES

White Wagtail   *Motacilla alba*

DATE

LOCALITY

HABITAT

NOTES

Black-backed Wagtail   *Motacilla lugens*

DATE

LOCALITY

HABITAT

NOTES

Brown Tree-Pipit   *Anthus trivialis*

DATE

LOCALITY

HABITAT

NOTES

Olive Tree-Pipit   *Anthus hodgsoni*

DATE

LOCALITY

HABITAT

NOTES

Pechora Pipit   *Anthus gustavi*

DATE

LOCALITY

HABITAT

NOTES

Red-throated Pipit   *Anthus cervinus*

DATE

LOCALITY

HABITAT

NOTES

Water Pipit   *Anthus spinoletta*

DATE

LOCALITY

HABITAT

NOTES

Sprague's Pipit   *Anthus spragueii*

DATE

LOCALITY

HABITAT

NOTES

Waxwings *(Bombycillidae)*

Bohemina Waxwing   *Bombycilla garrulus*

DATE

LOCALITY

HABITAT

NOTES

Cedar Waxwing   *Bombycilla cedrorum*

DATE

LOCALITY

HABITAT

NOTES

Silky Flycatchers (*Ptilogonatidae*)

Phainopepla   *Phainopepla nitens*

DATE

LOCALITY

HABITAT

NOTES

Shrikes (*Laniidae*)

Brown Shrike   *Lanius cristatus*

DATE

LOCALITY

HABITAT

NOTES

Northern Shrike   *Lanius excubitor*

DATE

LOCALITY

HABITAT

NOTES

Loggerhead Shrike   *Lanius ludovicianus*

DATE

LOCALITY

HABITAT

NOTES

Starlings and Allies (*Sturnidae*)

European Starling   *Sturnus vulgaris*

DATE

LOCALITY

HABITAT

NOTES

Crested Myna   *Acridotheres cristatellus*

DATE

LOCALITY

HABITAT

NOTES

Vireos (*Vireonidae*)

White-eyed Vireo   *Vireo griseus*

DATE

LOCALITY

HABITAT

NOTES

Bell's Vireo   *Vireo bellii*

DATE

LOCALITY

HABITAT

NOTES

Black-capped Vireo   *Vireo atricapillus*

DATE

LOCALITY

HABITAT

NOTES

Gray Vireo   *Vireo vicinior*

DATE

LOCALITY

HABITAT

NOTES

Solitary Vireo   *Vireo solitarius*

DATE

LOCALITY

HABITAT

NOTES

Yellow-throated Vireo · *Vireo flavifrons*

DATE

LOCALITY

HABITAT

NOTES

Hutton's Vireo · *Vireo huttoni*

DATE

LOCALITY

HABITAT

NOTES

Warbling Vireo · *Vireo gilvus*

DATE

LOCALITY

HABITAT

NOTES

Philadelphia Vireo · *Vireo philadelphicus*

DATE

LOCALITY

HABITAT

NOTES

Red-eyed Vireo   *Vireo olivaceus*

DATE

LOCALITY

HABITAT

NOTES

Black-whiskered Vireo   *Vireo altiloquus*

DATE

LOCALITY

HABITAT

NOTES

Wood Warblers; Bananaquits; Tanagers; Cardinals & Grosbeaks; Sparrows; Blackbirds; and Allies *(Emberizidae)*

Bachman's Warbler   *Vermivora bachmanii*

DATE

LOCALITY

HABITAT

NOTES

Blue-winged Warbler   *Vermivora pinus*

DATE

LOCALITY

HABITAT

NOTES

Golden-winged Warbler   *Vermivora chrysoptera*

DATE

LOCALITY

HABITAT

NOTES

Tennessee Warbler   *Vermivora peregrina*

DATE

LOCALITY

HABITAT

NOTES

Orange-crowned Warbler   *Vermivora celata*

DATE

LOCALITY

HABITAT

NOTES

Nashville Warbler   *Vermivora ruficapilla*

DATE

LOCALITY

HABITAT

NOTES

Virginia's Warbler *Vermivora virginiae*

DATE

LOCALITY

HABITAT

NOTES

Colima Warbler *Vermivora crissalis*

DATE

LOCALITY

HABITAT

NOTES

Lucy's Warbler *Vermivora luciae*

DATE

LOCALITY

HABITAT

NOTES

Northern Parula *Parula americana*

DATE

LOCALITY

HABITAT

NOTES

Tropical Parula   *Parula pitiayumi*

DATE

LOCALITY

HABITAT

NOTES

Crescent-chested Warbler   *Vermivora superciliosa*

DATE

LOCALITY

HABITAT

NOTES

Yellow Warbler   *Dendroica petechia*

DATE

LOCALITY

HABITAT

NOTES

Chestnut-sided Warbler   *Dendroica pensylvanica*

DATE

LOCALITY

HABITAT

NOTES

Magnolia Warbler — *Dendroica magnolia*

DATE

LOCALITY

HABITAT

NOTES

Cape May Warbler — *Dendroica tigrina*

DATE

LOCALITY

HABITAT

NOTES

Black-throated Blue Warbler — *Dendroica caerulescens*

DATE

LOCALITY

HABITAT

NOTES

Yellow-rumped Warbler — *Dendroica coronata*

DATE

LOCALITY

HABITAT

NOTES

Black-throated Gray Warbler *Dendroica nigrescens*

DATE

LOCALITY

HABITAT

NOTES

Townsend's Warbler   *Dendroica townsendi*

DATE

LOCALITY

HABITAT

NOTES

Hermit Warbler   *Dendroica occidentalis*

DATE

LOCALITY

HABITAT

NOTES

Black-throated Green Warbler
Dendroica virens

DATE

LOCALITY

HABITAT

NOTES

Golden-cheeked Warbler   *Dendroica chrysoparia*

DATE

LOCALITY

HABITAT

NOTES

Blackburnian Warbler   *Dendroica fusca*

DATE

LOCALITY

HABITAT

NOTES

Yellow-throated Warbler   *Dendroica dominica*

DATE

LOCALITY

HABITAT

NOTES

Grace's Warbler   *Dendroica graciae*

DATE

LOCALITY

HABITAT

NOTES

Pine Warbler   *Dendroica pinus*

DATE

LOCALITY

HABITAT

NOTES

Kirtland's Warbler   *Dendroica kirtlandii*

DATE

LOCALITY

HABITAT

NOTES

Prairie Warbler   *Dendroica discolor*

DATE

LOCALITY

HABITAT

NOTES

Palm Warbler   *Dendroica palmarum*

DATE

LOCALITY

HABITAT

NOTES

Bay-breasted Warbler   *Dendroica castanea*

DATE

LOCALITY

HABITAT

NOTES

Blackpoll Warbler   *Dendroica striata*

DATE

LOCALITY

HABITAT

NOTES

Cerulean Warbler   *Dendroica cerulea*

DATE

LOCALITY

HABITAT

NOTES

Black-and-white Warbler   *Mniotilta varia*

DATE

LOCALITY

HABITAT

NOTES

American Redstart   *Setophaga ruticilla*

DATE

LOCALITY

HABITAT

NOTES

Prothonotary Warbler   *Protonotaria citrea*

DATE

LOCALITY

HABITAT

NOTES

Worm-eating Warbler   *Helmitheros vermivorus*

DATE

LOCALITY

HABITAT

NOTES

Swainson's Warbler   *Limnothlypis swainsonii*

DATE

LOCALITY

HABITAT

NOTES

Ovenbird   *Seiurus autrocapillus*

DATE

LOCALITY

HABITAT

NOTES

Northern Waterthrush   *Seiurus noveboracensis*

DATE

LOCALITY

HABITAT

NOTES

Louisiana Waterthrush   *Seiurus motacilla*

DATE

LOCALITY

HABITAT

NOTES

Kentucky Warbler   *Oporornis formosus*

DATE

LOCALITY

HABITAT

NOTES

Connecticut Warbler   *Oporornis agilis*

DATE

LOCALITY

HABITAT

NOTES

Mourning Warbler   *Oporornis philadelphia*

DATE

LOCALITY

HABITAT

NOTES

MacGillivray's Warbler   *Oporornis tolmiei*

DATE

LOCALITY

HABITAT

NOTES

Common Yellowthroat   *Geothlypis trichas*

DATE

LOCALITY

HABITAT

NOTES

Gray-crowned Yellowthroat
Geothlypis poliocephala

DATE

LOCALITY

HABITAT

NOTES

Hooded Warbler   *Wilsonia citrina*

DATE

LOCALITY

HABITAT

NOTES

Wilson's Warbler   *Wilsonia pusilla*

DATE

LOCALITY

HABITAT

NOTES

Canada Warbler   *Wilsonia canadensis*

DATE

LOCALITY

HABITAT

NOTES

Red-faced Warbler   *Cardellina rubrifrons*

DATE

LOCALITY

HABITAT

NOTES

Painted Redstart   *Myioborus pictus*

DATE

LOCALITY

HABITAT

NOTES

Slate-throated Redstart   *Myioborus miniatus*

DATE

LOCALITY

HABITAT

NOTES

Fan-tailed Warbler   *Euthlypis lachrymosa*

DATE

LOCALITY

HABITAT

NOTES

Golden-crowned Warbler
Basileuterus culicivorus

DATE

LOCALITY

HABITAT

NOTES

Rufous-capped Warbler   *Basileuterus rufifrons*

DATE

LOCALITY

HABITAT

NOTES

Yellow-breasted Chat   *Icteria virens*

DATE

LOCALITY

HABITAT

NOTES

Olive Warbler   *Peucedramus taeniatus*

DATE

LOCALITY

HABITAT

NOTES

Bananaquit   *Coereba flaveola*

DATE

LOCALITY

HABITAT

NOTES

Stripe-headed Tanager   *Spindalis zena*

DATE

LOCALITY

HABITAT

NOTES

Hepatic Tanager   *Piranga flava*

DATE

LOCALITY

HABITAT

NOTES

Summer Tanager   *Piranga rubra*

DATE

LOCALITY

HABITAT

NOTES

Scarlet Tanager   *Piranga olivacea*

DATE

LOCALITY

HABITAT

NOTES

Western Tanager   *Piranga ludoviciana*

DATE

LOCALITY

HABITAT

NOTES

Crimson-collared Grosbeak

Rhodothraupus celaeno

DATE

LOCALITY

HABITAT

NOTES

Northern Cardinal   *Cardinalis cardinalis*

DATE

LOCALITY

HABITAT

NOTES

Pyrrhuloxia   *Cardinalis sinuatus*

DATE

LOCALITY

HABITAT

NOTES

Yellow Grosbeak   *Pheucticus chrysopeplus*

DATE

LOCALITY

HABITAT

NOTES

Rose-breasted Grosbeak   *Pheucticus ludovicianus*

DATE

LOCALITY

HABITAT

NOTES

Black-headed Grosbeak
Pheucticus melanocephalus

DATE

LOCALITY

HABITAT

NOTES

Blue Bunting   *Cyanocompsa parellina*

DATE

LOCALITY

HABITAT

NOTES

Blue Grosbeak   *Guiraca caerulea*

DATE

LOCALITY

HABITAT

NOTES

Lazuli Bunting   *Passerina amoena*

DATE

LOCALITY

HABITAT

NOTES

Indigo Bunting   *Passerina cyanea*

DATE

LOCALITY

HABITAT

NOTES

Varied Bunting   *Passerina versicolor*

DATE

LOCALITY

HABITAT

NOTES

Painted Bunting   *Passerina ciris*

DATE

LOCALITY

HABITAT

NOTES

Dickcissel   *Spiza americana*

DATE

LOCALITY

HABITAT

NOTES

Olive Sparrow   *Arremonops rufivirgatus*

DATE

LOCALITY

HABITAT

NOTES

Green-tailed Towhee   *Pipilo chlorurus*

DATE

LOCALITY

HABITAT

NOTES

Rufous-sided Towhee   *Pipilo erythrophthalmus*

DATE

LOCALITY

HABITAT

NOTES

Brown Towhee   *Pipilo fuscus*

DATE

LOCALITY

HABITAT

NOTES

Abert's Towhee   *Pipilo aberti*

DATE

LOCALITY

HABITAT

NOTES

White-collared Seedeater   *Sporophila torqueola*

DATE

LOCALITY

HABITAT

NOTES

Black-faced Grassquit   *Tiaris bicolor*

DATE

LOCALITY

HABITAT

NOTES

Bachman's Sparrow   *Aimophila aestivalis*

DATE

LOCALITY

HABITAT

NOTES

Botteri's Sparrow   *Aimophila botterii*

DATE

LOCALITY

HABITAT

NOTES

Cassin's Sparrow   *Aimophila cassinii*

DATE

LOCALITY

HABITAT

NOTES

Rufous-winged Sparrow   *Aimophila carpalis*

DATE

LOCALITY

HABITAT

NOTES

Rufous-crowned Sparrow   *Aimophila ruficeps*

DATE

LOCALITY

HABITAT

NOTES

American Tree Sparrow   *Spizella arborea*

DATE

LOCALITY

HABITAT

NOTES

Chipping Sparrow   *Spizella passerina*

DATE

LOCALITY

HABITAT

NOTES

Clay-colored Sparrow   *Spizella pallida*

DATE

LOCALITY

HABITAT

NOTES

Brewer's Sparrow   *Spizella breweri*

DATE

LOCALITY

HABITAT

NOTES

Field Sparrow   *Spizella pusilla*

DATE

LOCALITY

HABITAT

NOTES

Black-chinned Sparrow   *Spizella atrogularis*

DATE

LOCALITY

HABITAT

NOTES

Vesper Sparrow   *Pooecetes gramineus*

DATE

LOCALITY

HABITAT

NOTES

Lark Sparrow   *Chondestes grammacus*

DATE

LOCALITY

HABITAT

NOTES

Black-throated Sparrow   *Amphispiza bilineata*

DATE

LOCALITY

HABITAT

NOTES

Sage Sparrow — *Amphispiza belli*

DATE

LOCALITY

HABITAT

NOTES

Five-striped Sparrow — *Amphispiza quinquestriata*

DATE

LOCALITY

HABITAT

NOTES

Lark Bunting — *Calamospiza melanocorys*

DATE

LOCALITY

HABITAT

NOTES

Savannah Sparrow — *Passerculus sandwichensis*

DATE

LOCALITY

HABITAT

NOTES

Baird's Sparrow   *Ammodramus bairdii*

DATE

LOCALITY

HABITAT

NOTES

Grasshopper Sparrow
                                Ammodramus savannarum

DATE

LOCALITY

HABITAT

NOTES

Henslow's Sparrow   *Ammodramus henslowii*

DATE

LOCALITY

HABITAT

NOTES

Le Conte's Sparrow   *Ammodramus leconteii*

DATE

LOCALITY

HABITAT

NOTES

Sharp-tailed Sparrow   *Ammodramus caudacutus*

DATE

LOCALITY

HABITAT

NOTES

Seaside Sparrow   *Ammodramus maritimus*

DATE

LOCALITY

HABITAT

NOTES

Fox Sparrow   *Passerella iliaca*

DATE

LOCALITY

HABITAT

NOTES

Song Sparrow   *Melospiza melodia*

DATE

LOCALITY

HABITAT

NOTES

Lincoln's Sparrow   *Melospiza lincolnii*

DATE

LOCALITY

HABITAT

NOTES

Swamp Sparrow   *Melospiza georgiana*

DATE

LOCALITY

HABITAT

NOTES

White-throated Sparrow   *Zonotrichia albicollis*

DATE

LOCALITY

HABITAT

NOTES

Golden-crowned Sparrow   *Zonotrichia atricapilla*

DATE

LOCALITY

HABITAT

NOTES

White-crowned Sparrow   *Zonotrichia leucophrys*

DATE

LOCALITY

HABITAT

NOTES

Harris' Sparrow   *Zonotrichia querula*

DATE

LOCALITY

HABITAT

NOTES

Dark-eyed Junco   *Junco hyemalis*

DATE

LOCALITY

HABITAT

NOTES

Yellow-eyed Junco   *Junco phaeonotus*

DATE

LOCALITY

HABITAT

NOTES

McCown's Longspur   *Calcarius mccownii*

DATE

LOCALITY

HABITAT

NOTES

Lapland Longspur   *Calcarius lapponicus*

DATE

LOCALITY

HABITAT

NOTES

Smith's Longspur   *Calcarius pictus*

DATE

LOCALITY

HABITAT

NOTES

Chestnut-collared Longspur   *Calcarius ornatus*

DATE

LOCALITY

HABITAT

NOTES

Little Bunting   *Emberiza pusilla*

DATE

LOCALITY

HABITAT

NOTES

Rustic Bunting   *Emberiza rustica*

DATE

LOCALITY

HABITAT

NOTES

Gray Bunting   *Emberiza variabilis*

DATE

LOCALITY

HABITAT

NOTES

Pallas' Reed-Bunting   *Emberiza pallasi*

DATE

LOCALITY

HABITAT

NOTES

Common Reed-Bunting *Emberiza schoeniclus*

DATE

LOCALITY

HABITAT

NOTES

Snow Bunting *Plectrophenax nivalis*

DATE

LOCALITY

HABITAT

NOTES

McKay's Bunting *Plectrophenax hyperboreus*

DATE

LOCALITY

HABITAT

NOTES

Bobolink *Dolichonyx oryzivorus*

DATE

LOCALITY

HABITAT

NOTES

Red-winged Blackbird *Agelaius phoeniceus*

DATE

LOCALITY

HABITAT

NOTES

Tricolored Blackbird *Agelaius tricolor*

DATE

LOCALITY

HABITAT

NOTES

Tawny-shouldered Blackbird

Agelaius humeralis

DATE

LOCALITY

HABITAT

NOTES

Eastern Meadowlark *Sturnella magna*

DATE

LOCALITY

HABITAT

NOTES

Western Meadowlark   *Sturnella neglecta*

DATE

LOCALITY

HABITAT

NOTES

Yellow-headed Blackbird
Xanthocephalus xanthocephalus

DATE

LOCALITY

HABITAT

NOTES

Rusty Blackbird   *Euphagus carolinus*

DATE

LOCALITY

HABITAT

NOTES

Brewer's Blackbird   *Euphagus cyanocephalus*

DATE

LOCALITY

HABITAT

NOTES

Great-tailed Grackle   *Quiscalus mexicanus*

DATE

LOCALITY

HABITAT

NOTES

Boat-tailed Grackle   *Quiscalus major*

DATE

LOCALITY

HABITAT

NOTES

Common Gracle   *Quiscalus quiscula*

DATE

LOCALITY

HABITAT

NOTES

Bronzed Cowbird   *Molothrus aeneus*

DATE

LOCALITY

HABITAT

NOTES

Brown-headed Cowbird   *Molothrus ater*

DATE

LOCALITY

HABITAT

NOTES

Black-vented Oriole   *Icterus wagleri*

DATE

LOCALITY

HABITAT

NOTES

Orchard Oriole   *Icterus spurius*

DATE

LOCALITY

HABITAT

NOTES

Hooded Oriole   *Icterus cucullatus*

DATE

LOCALITY

HABITAT

NOTES

Streak-backed Oriole   *Icterus pustulatus*

DATE

LOCALITY

HABITAT

NOTES

Spot-breasted Oriole   *Icterus pectoralis*

DATE

LOCALITY

HABITAT

NOTES

Altamira Oriole   *Icterus gularis*

DATE

LOCALITY

HABITAT

NOTES

Audubon's Oriole   *Icterus graduacauda*

DATE

LOCALITY

HABITAT

NOTES

Northern Oriole   *Icterus galbula*

DATE

LOCALITY

HABITAT

NOTES

Scott's Oriole   *Icterus parisorum*

DATE

LOCALITY

HABITAT

NOTES

Finches and Allies *(Fringillidae)*

Common Chaffinch   *Fringilla coelebs*

DATE

LOCALITY

HABITAT

NOTES

Brambling   *Fringilla montifringilla*

DATE

LOCALITY

HABITAT

NOTES

Rosy Finch   *Leucosticte arctoa*

DATE

LOCALITY

HABITAT

NOTES

Pine Grosbeak   *Pinicola enucleator*

DATE

LOCALITY

HABITAT

NOTES

Common Rosefinch   *Carpodacus erythrinus*

DATE

LOCALITY

HABITAT

NOTES

Purple Finch   *Carpodacus purpureus*

DATE

LOCALITY

HABITAT

NOTES

Cassin's Finch   *Carpodacus cassinii*

DATE

LOCALITY

HABITAT

NOTES

House Finch   *Carpodacus mexicanus*

DATE

LOCALITY

HABITAT

NOTES

Red Crossbill   *Loxia curvirostra*

DATE

LOCALITY

HABITAT

NOTES

White-winged Crossbill   *Loxia leucoptera*

DATE

LOCALITY

HABITAT

NOTES

Common Redpoll *Carduelis flammea*

DATE

LOCALITY

HABITAT

NOTES

Hoary Redpoll *Carduelis hornemanni*

DATE

LOCALITY

HABITAT

NOTES

Pine Siskin *Carduelis pinus*

DATE

LOCALITY

HABITAT

NOTES

Lesser Goldfinch *Carduelis psaltria*

DATE

LOCALITY

HABITAT

NOTES

Lawrence's Goldfinch   *Carduelis lawrencei*

DATE

LOCALITY

HABITAT

NOTES

American Goldfinch   *Carduelis tristis*

DATE

LOCALITY

HABITAT

NOTES

Oriental Greenfinch   *Carduelis sinica*

DATE

LOCALITY

HABITAT

NOTES

Eurasian Bullfinch   *Pyrrhula pyrrhula*

DATE

LOCALITY

HABITAT

NOTES

Evening Grosbeak   *Coccothraustes vespertinus*

DATE

LOCALITY

HABITAT

NOTES

Hawfinch   *Coccothraustes coccothraustes*

DATE

LOCALITY

HABITAT

NOTES

Old World Sparrows (*Passeridae*)

House Sparrow   *Passer domesticus*

DATE

LOCALITY

HABITAT

NOTES

Eurasian Tree Sparrow   *Passer montanus*

DATE

LOCALITY

HABITAT

NOTES

Bibliography

Alden, Peter, and John Gooders. *Finding Birds Around the World.* Boston: Houghton Mifflin Co., 1981.

Cronin, Edward W., Jr. *Getting Started in Bird Watching.* Boston: Houghton Mifflin Co., 1986.

Dennis, John V. *A Complete Guide to Bird Feeding.* New York: Alfred A. Knopf, 1984.

Farrand, John, Jr., Editor. *Audubon Society Master Guide to Birding.* 3 Vols. New York: Alfred A. Knopf, Inc., 1983.

Geffen, Alice M. *A Birdwatcher's Guide to the Eastern United States.* New York: Barron's/Woodbury, 1978.

Godfrey, W. Earl. *The Birds of Canada.* Ottawa: National Museums of Canada, 1979.

Griscom, Ludlow, and Alexander Sprunt, Jr. *The Warblers of America.* Garden City, New York: Doubleday & Co., Inc., 1979.

Harrison, Colin. *A Field Guide to the Nests, Eggs and Nestlings of North American Birds.* Cleveland: Collins, 1978.

Harrison, George H. *Roger Tory Peterson's Dozen Birding Hot Spots.* New York: Simon & Schuster, Inc., 1976.

_____. *The Backyard Bird Watcher.* New York: Simon & Schuster, Inc., 1979.

Harrison, Hal. H. *Wood Warblers' World.* New York: Simon & Schuster, Inc., 1984.

Harrison, Peter. *Seabirds—An Identification Guide.* Boston: Houghton Mifflin Co., 1983.

_____. *A Field Guide to Seabirds of the World.* Lexington, Massachusetts: The Stephen Greene Press, 1987.

Hayman, Peter, John Marchant, and Tony Prater. *Shorebirds—An Identification Guide.* Boston: Houghton Mifflin Co., 1986.

Hickey, Joseph J. *A Guide to Bird Watching.* New York: Dover Publications, 1975.

Johnsgard, Paul A. *Waterfowl of North America.* Bloomington and London: Indiana University Press, 1975.

Kastner, Joseph. *A World of Watchers.* San Francisco: Sierra Club Books, 1986.

Kitching, Jessie. *Birdwatcher's Guide to Wildlife Sanctuaries.* New York: Arco Publishing Co., Inc. 1976.

Laycock, Geroge. *The Birdwatcher's Bible.* Garden City, New York: Doubleday & Co., Inc., 1976.

Lentz, Joan Easton, and Judith Young. *Birdwatching—A Guide for Beginners.* Santa Barbara, California: Capra Press, 1985.

Lotz, Aileen R. *Birding Around the World.* New York: Dodd, Mead & Co., 1987.

McElroy, Thomas P. *The Habitat Guide to Birding.* New York: Alfred A. Knopf, 1974.

National Geographic Society. *Field Guide to the Birds of North America.* Washington, D.C., 1987.

Peterson, Roger Tory. *A Field Guide to the Birds of Texas—and Adjacent States.* Boston: Houghton Mifflin Co., 1963.

——. *A Field Guide to Western Birds.* Second Edition. Boston: Houghton Mifflin Co., 1969.

——. *A Field Guide to the Birds—East of the Rockies.* Fourth Edition. Boston: Houghton Mifflin Co., 1980.

Pettengill, Olin Sewall, Jr. *A Guide to Bird Finding—East of the Mississippi.* Second Edition. New York: Oxford University Press, 1977.

——. *A Guide to Bird Finding—West of the Mississippi.* Second Edition. New York: Oxford University Press, 1981.

Piatt, Jean. *Adventures in Birding—Confessions of a Lister.* New York: Alfred A. Knopf, 1973.

Robbins, Chandler S., Bertel Brunn and Herbert S. Zim. *Birds of North America—A Guide to Field Identification.* Revised Edition. New York: Golden Press, 1983.

Socha, Laura O'Biso. *A Bird Watcher's Handbook.* New York: Dodd, Mead and Co., 1987.

Stokes, Donald W., And Lillian Q. *A Guide to Bird Behavior.* 3 Vols. Boston and Toronto: Little, Brown & Co., 1979.

Terres, John K. *The Audubon Society Encyclopedia of North American Birds.* New York: Alfred A. Knopf, 1980.

Tyrrell, Robert A., and Esther Quesada. *Hummingbirds—Their Life and Behavior.* New York: Crown Publishers, Inc., 1985.

Zimmer, Kevin J. *The Western Bird Watcher.* Englewood Cliffs, New Jersey: Prentice-Hall, Inc., 1985.

Accentor, Siberian, 159
Accipiter cooperii, 40
   gentilis, 41
   striatus, 40
Accipitridae, 38
Acridotheres cristatellus, 163
Actitis hypoleucos, 64
   macularia, 64
Aechmophorus occidentalis, 4
Aegithalidae, 143
Aegolius acadicus, 106
   funereus, 106
Aeronautes saxatalis, 110
Aethia cristatella, 92
   pusilla, 92
   pygmaea, 92
Agelaius humeralis, 199
   phoeniceus, 199
   tricolor, 199
Aimophila aestivalis, 187
   botterii, 187
   carpalis, 188
   cassinii, 188
   ruficeps, 188
Aix sponsa, 26
Ajaia ajaja, 21
Alauda arvensis, 133
Alaudidae, 133
Albatross, Black-browed, 5
   Black-footed, 4
   Laysan, 5
   Short-tailed, 4
   Shy, 5
   Yellow-nosed, 5
Alca Torda, 89
Alcendinidae, 117
Alcidae, 88
Alectoris chukar, 47
Alle alle, 88
Amazilia beryllina, 112
   tzacatl, 112
   violiceps, 112
   yucatanensis, 112
Amazona oratrix, 99
   viridigenalis, 99

Ammodramus bairdii, 192
   caudacutus, 193
   henslowii, 192
   leconteii, 192
   maritimus, 193
   savannarum, 192
Amphispiza belli, 191
   bilineata, 190
   quinquestriata, 191
Anas acuta, 29
   americana, 30
   bahamensis, 28
   clypeata, 30
   crecca, 27
   cyanoptera, 29
   discors, 29
   falcata, 27
   formosa, 27
   fulvigula, 28
   penelope, 30
   platyrhynchos, 28
   poecilorhyncha, 28
   querquedula, 29
   rubripes, 27
   strepera, 30
Anatidae, 22
Anhinga, 16
Anhinga anhinga, 16
Anhingidae, 16
Ani, Groove-billed, 101
   Smooth-billed, 101
Anous minutus, 88
   stolidus, 88
Anser albifrons, 25
   brachyrhynchus, 24
   erythropus, 24
   fabalis, 24
Anthus cervinus, 161
   gustavi, 160
   hodgsoni, 160
   spinoletta, 161
   spragueii, 161
   trivialis, 160
Aphelocoma coerulescens, 138
   ultramarina, 138

Aphriza virgata, 68
Apodidae, 108
Apus apus, 110
   pacificus, 110
Aquila chrysaetos, 44
Aramidae, 55
Aramus guarauna, 55
Archilochus alexandri, 114
   colubris, 114
Ardea herodias, 17
Ardeidae, 17
Arenaria interpres, 68
   melanocephala, 68
Arremonops rufivirgatus, 185
Asio flammeus, 105
   otus, 105
Athene cunicularia, 104
Atthis heloisa, 115
Auklet, Cassin's, 91
   Crested, 92
   Least, 92
   Parakeet, 91
   Rhinoceros, 92
   Whiskered, 92
Auriparus flaviceps, 143
Avocet, American, 61
Aythya affinis, 32
   americana, 31
   collaris, 31
   ferina, 31
   fuligula, 32
   marila, 32
   valisineria, 31

Bananaquit, 181
Bartramia longicauda, 65
Basileuterus culicivorus, 180
   rufifrons, 180
Becard, Rose-throated, 132
Bittern, American, 17
   Least, 17
Blackbird, Brewer's, 200
   Red-winged, 199
   Rusty, 200
   Tawny-shouldered, 199

   Tricolored, 199
   Yellow-headed, 200
Bluebird, Eastern, 151
   Mountain, 152
   Western, 152
Bluethroat, 151
Bobolink, 198
Bobwhite, Northern, 51
Bombycilla cedrorum, 162
   garrulus, 161
Bombycillidae, 161
Bonasa umbellus, 49
Booby, Blue-footed, 13
   Brown, 13
   Masked, 13
   Red-footed, 13
Botaurus lentiginosus, 17
Brachyramphus brevirostris, 90
   marmoratus, 90
Brambling, 204
Brant, 26
Branta bernicla, 26
   canadensis, 26
   leucopsis, 26
Brotogeris versicolurus, 98
Bubo virginianus, 103
Bubulcus ibis, 19
Bucephala albeola, 35
   clangula, 35
   islandica, 35
Budgerigar, 97
Bufflehead, 35
Bulbul, Red-whiskered, 145
Bullfinch, Eurasian, 208
Bunting, Blue, 184
Bunting, Common Reed-, 198
   Gray, 197
   Indigo, 184
   Lark, 191
   Lazuli, 184
   Little, 197
   McKay's, 198
   Painted, 185
   Palas' Reed-, 197
   Rustic, 197

Snow, 198
Varied, 185
Burhinidae, 56
Burhinus bistriatus, 56
Bushtit, 143
Buteo albicaudatus, 43
    albonotatus, 43
    brachyurus, 42
    jamaicensis, 43
    lagopus, 44
    lineatus, 42
    magnirostris, 42
    nitidus, 41
    platypterus, 42
    regalis, 44
    swainsoni, 43
Buteogallus anthracinus, 41
Butorides striatus, 20

Calamospiza melanocorys, 191
Calcarius lapponicus, 196
    mccownii, 196
    ornatus, 196
    pictus, 196
Calidris acuminata, 72
    alba, 69
    alpina, 73
    bairdii, 71
    canutus, 69
    ferruginea, 73
    fuscicollis, 71
    himantopus, 73
    maritima, 72
    mauri, 70
    melanotos, 72
    minuta, 70
    minutilla, 71
    ptilocnemis, 72
    pusilla, 69
    ruficollis, 70
    subminuta, 71
    temminckii, 70
    tenuirostris, 69
Callipepla californica, 51
    gambelii, 51

    squamata, 51
Calliphlox evelynae, 113
Calonectris diomedea, 7
    leucomelas, 6
Calothorax lucifer, 114
Calypte anna, 114
    costae, 115
Campephilus principalis, 123
Camptostoma imberbe, 123
Campylorhynchus brunneicapillus, 145
Canvasback, 31
Caprimulgidae, 106
Caprimulgus carolinensis, 107
    indicus, 108
    ridgwayi, 108
    vociferus, 108
Caracara, Crested, 44
Cardellina rubrifrons, 179
Cardinal, Northern, 182
Cardinalis cardinalis, 182
    sinuatus, 183
Carduelis flammea, 207
    hornemanni, 207
    lawrencei, 208
    pinus, 207
    psaltria, 207
    sinica, 208
    tristis, 208
Carpodacus cassinii, 206
    erythrinus, 205
    mexicanus, 206
    purpureus, 205
Casmerodius albus, 18
Catbird, Gray, 156
Catharacta maccormicki, 78
    skua, 77
Cathartes aura, 37
Cathartidae, 37
Catharus fuscescens, 152
    guttatus, 153
    minimus, 153
    ustulatus, 153
Catherpes mexicanus, 146
Catoptrophorus semipalmatus, 63
Centrocercus urophasianus, 49

Cepphus columba, 90
  grylle, 89
Cerorhinca monocerata, 92
Certhia americana, 145
Certhiidae, 145
Ceryle alcyon, 117
  torquata, 117
Chachalaca, Plain, 46
Chaetura pelagica, 109
  vauxi, 109
Chaffinch, Common, 204
Chamaea fasciata, 156
Charadriidae, 57
Charadrius alexandrinus, 58
  dubius, 59
  hiaticula, 58
  melodus, 59
  mongolus, 58
  montanus, 60
  morinellus, 60
  semipalmatus, 59
  vociferus, 59
  wilsonia, 58
Chat, Yellow-breasted, 180
Chen caerulescens, 25
  canagica, 25
  rossii, 25
Chickadee, Black-capped, 141
  Boreal, 142
  Carolina, 141
  Chestnut-backed, 142
  Mexican, 141
  Mountain, 141
Chlidonias leucopterus, 87
  niger, 87
Chloroceryle americana, 117
Chlorostilbon ricordii, 111
Chondestes grammacus, 190
Chondrohierax uncinatus, 38
Chordeiles acutipennis, 106
  gundlachii, 107
  minor, 106
Chuck-will's-widow, 107
Chukar, 47
Ciconiidae, 22

Cinclus mexicanus, 147
Circus cyaneus, 40
Cistothorus palustris, 147
  platensis, 147
Clangula hyemalis, 34
Coccothraustes coccothraustes, 209
  vespertinus, 209
Coccyzus americanus, 100
  erythropthalmus, 100
  minor, 100
Coereba flaveola, 181
Colaptes auratus, 122
Colibri thalassinus, 111
Colinus virginianus, 51
Columba fasciata, 94
  flavirostris, 94
  leucocephala, 94
  livia, 93
  squamosa, 94
Columbidae, 93
Columbina inca, 96
  passerina, 96
  talpacoti, 96
Condor, Califorina 37
Contopus borealis, 123
  pertinax, 124
  sordidulus, 124
  virens, 124
Coot, American, 55
  Caribbean, 55
  Eurasian, 55
Coragyps atratus, 37
Cormorant, Brandt's, 15
  Double-crested, 15
  Great, 14
  Olivaceous, 15
  Pelagic, 15
  Red-faced 16
Corvidae, 136
Corvus brachyrhynochos, 139
  caurinus, 139
  corax, 140
  cryptoleucus, 140
  imparatus, 140
  ossifragus, 140

Coturnicops noveboracensis, 52
Cowbird, Bronzed, 201
   Brown-headed, 202
Cracidae, 46
Crake, Corn, 52
   Paint-billed, 54
Crane, Common, 56
   Sandhill, 56
   Whooping, 56
Creeper, Brown, 145
Crex crex, 52
Crossbill, Red, 206
   White-winged, 206
Croptophaga ani, 101
   sulcirostris, 101
Crow, American, 139
   Fish, 140
   Mexican, 140
   Northwestern, 139
Cuckoo, Black-billed, 100
   Common, 99
   Mangrove, 100
   Oriental, 99
   Yellow-billed, 100
Cuculidae, 99
Cuculus canorus, 99
   saturatus, 99
Curlew, Bristle-thighed, 66
   Eskimo, 65
   Eurasian, 66
   Far Eastern, 66
   Little, 65
   Long-billed, 67
   Slender-billed, 66
Cyanocitta cristata, 137
   stelleri, 137
Cyanocompsa parellina, 184
Cyanocorax morio, 137
   yncas, 137
Cyclorrhynchus psittacula, 91
Cygnus buccinator, 23
   columbianus, 23
   cygnus, 23
   olor, 24
Cynanthus latirostris, 111

Cypseloides niger, 108
Cyrtonyx montezumae, 50

Delichon urbica, 136
Dendragapus canadensis, 48
   obscurus, 48
Dendrocygna bicolor, 22
   autumnalis, 23
Dendroica caerulescens, 170
   castanea, 174
   cerulea, 174
   chrysoparia, 172
   coronata, 170
   discolor, 173
   dominica, 172
   fusca, 172
   graciae, 172
   kirtlandii, 173
   mangolia, 170
   nigrescens, 171
   occidentalis, 171
   palmarum, 173
   pensylvanica, 169
   petechia, 169
   pinus, 173
   striata, 174
   tigrina, 170
   townsendi, 171
   virens, 171
Dickcissel, 185
Diomedea albatrus, 4
   cauta, 5
   chlororhynchos, 5
   immutabilis, 5
   melanophris, 5
   nigripes, 4
Diomedeidae, 4
Dipper, American 147
Dolichonyx oryzivorus, 198
Dotterel, Eurasian, 60
Dove, Common Ground-, 96
   Inca, 96
   Key West Quail-, 97
   Mourning, 96
   Ringed Turtle-, 95

Rock, 93
Ruddy Ground-, 96
Ruddy Quail-, 97
Spotted, 95
White-tipped, 97
White-winged, 95
Zenaida, 95
Dovekie, 88
Dowitcher, Long-billed, 75
Short-billed, 74
Dryocopus pileatus, 123
Duck, American Black, 27
Black-bellied Whistling-, 23
Fulvous Whistling-, 22
Harlequin, 33
Masked, 37
Mottled, 28
Ring-necked, 31
Ruddy, 36
Spot-billed, 28
Tufted, 32
Wood, 26
Dumetella carolinensis, 156
Dunlin, 73

Eagle, Bald, 39
Golden, 44
Steller's Sea-, 40
White-tailed, 39
Egret, Cattle, 19
Chinese, 18
Great, 18
Little, 18
Reddish, 19
Snowy, 18
Egretta caerulea, 19
eulophotes, 18
garzetta, 18
rufescens, 19
thula, 18
tricolor, 19
Eider, Common, 32
King, 33
Spectacled, 33
Steller's 33

Elanoides forficatus, 38
Elanus caeruleus, 38
Emberiza pallasi, 197
pussilla, 197
rustica, 197
schoeniclus, 198
variabilis, 197
Emberizidae, 166
Emerald, Cuban, 111
Empidonax alnorum, 125
difficilis, 126
flaviventris, 124
fulvifrons, 127
hammondii, 126
minimus, 125
oberholseri, 126
traillii, 125
virescens, 125
wrightii, 126
Empidonomus varius, 130
Eremophila alpestris, 133
Eudocimus albus, 20
ruber, 21
Eugenes fulgens, 113
Euphagus carolinus, 200
cyanocephalus, 200
Euptilotus neoxenus, 116
Eurynorhynchos pygmeus, 73
Euthlypis lachrymosa, 179

Falco columbarius, 45
femoralis, 45
mexicanus, 46
peregrinus, 46
rusticolus, 46
sparverius, 45
tinnunculus, 45
Falcon, Aplomado, 45
Peregrine, 46
Prairie, 46
Falconidae, 44
Ficedula parva, 150
Fieldfare, 154
Finch, Cassin's 206
House, 206

Purple, 205
Rosy, 205
Flamingo, Greater, 22
Flicker, Northern, 122
Flycatcher, Acadian, 125
Alder, 125
Ash-throated, 128
Brown-crested, 129
Buff-breasted, 127
Dusky, 126
Dusky-capped, 128
Fork-tailed, 132
Gray, 126
Gray-spotted, 150
Great Crested, 128
Hammond's, 126
La Sagra's, 129
Least, 125
Olive-sided, 123
Red-breasted, 150
Scissor-tailed, 132
Siberian, 150
Sulphur-bellied, 129
Variegated, 130
Vermilion, 128
Western, 126
Willow, 125
Yellow-bellied, 124
Francolin, Black, 47
Francolinus francolinus, 47
Fratercula arctica, 93
cirrhata, 93
corniculata, 93
Fregata ariel, 17
magnificens, 16
minor, 16
Fregatidae, 16
Frigatebird, Great, 16
Lesser, 17
Magnificent, 16
Fringilla coelebs, 204
montifringilla, 204
Fringillidae, 204
Fulica americana, 55
atra, 55

caribaea, 55
Fulmar, Northern, 6
Fulmarus glacialis, 6

Gadwall, 30
Gallinago gallinago, 75
Gallinula chloropus, 54
Gallinule, Purple, 54
Gannet, Northern, 14
Garganey, 29
Gavia adamsii, 2
arctica, 2
immer, 2
stellata, 2
Gaviidae, 2
Geococcyx californianus, 100
Geogrygon chrysia, 97
Geothlypis poliocephala, 178
trichas, 177
Geotrygon chrysia, 97
montana, 97
Glaucidium brasilianum, 104
gnoma, 103
Gnatcatcher, Black-capped 150
Black-tailed, 149
Blue-gray, 149
Godwit, Bar-tailed, 67
Black-tailed, 67
Hudsonian, 67
Marbled, 68
Goldeneye, Barrow's, 35
Common, 35
Goldfinch, American, 208
Lawrence's, 208
Lesser, 207
Goose, Barnacle, 26
Bean, 24
Canada, 26
Emperor, 25
Greater White-fronted, 25
Lesser White-fronted, 24
Pink-footed, 24
Ross', 25
Snow, 25
Goshawk, Northern, 41

Grackle, Boat-tailed, 201
    Common, 201
    Great-tailed, 201
Grassquit, Black-faced, 187
Grebe, Eared, 4
    Horned, 3
    Least, 3
    Pied-billed, 3
    Red-necked, 3
    Western, 4
Greenfinch, Oriental, 208
Greenshank, Common, 61
Grosbeak, Black-headed, 183
    Blue, 184
    Crimson-collared, 182
    Evening, 209
    Pine, 205
    Rose-breasted, 183
    Yellow, 183
Grouse, Blue, 48
    Ruffed, 49
    Sage, 49
    Sharp-tailed, 50
    Spruce, 48
Gruidae, 56
Grus americana, 56
    canadensis, 56
    grus, 56
Guillemot, Black, 89
    Pigeon, 90
Guiraca caerulea, 184
Gull, Bonaparte's, 79
    California, 80
    Common Black-headed, 79
    Franklin's, 78
    Glaucous, 82
    Glaucous-winged, 82
    Great Black-backed, 82
    Heermann's, 79
    Herring, 80
    Iceland, 81
    Ivory, 84
    Laughing, 78
    Lesser Black-backed, 81
    Little, 78

    Mew, 79
    Ring-billed, 80
    Ross', 83
    Sabine's, 83
    Slaty-backed, 81
    Thayer's, 80
    Western, 82
    Yellow-footed, 81
Gymnogyps californianus, 37
Gymnorhinus cyanocephalus, 138
Gyrfalcon, 46

Haematopodidae, 60
Haematopus bachmani, 60
    palliatus, 60
Haliaeetus albicilla, 39
    leucocephalus, 39
    pelagicus, 40
Harrier, Northern, 40
Hawfinch, 209
Hawk, Broad-winged, 42
Hawk, Common Black-, 41
    Cooper's, 40
    Ferruginous, 44
    Gray, 41
    Harris', 41
    Red-shouldered, 42
    Red-tailed, 43
    Roadside, 42
    Rough-legged, 44
    Sharp-shinned, 40
    Short-tailed, 42
    Swainson's, 43
    White-tailed, 43
    Zone-tailed, 43
Heliomaster constantii, 113
Helmitheros vermivorus, 175
Heron, Black-crowned Night-, 20
    Great Blue, 17
    Green-backed, 20
    Little Blue, 19
    Tricolored, 19
    Yellow-crowned Night-, 20
Heteroscelus brevipes, 64
    incanus, 63

Himantopus mexicanus, 61
Hirundapus caudacutus, 109
Hirundinidae, 133
Hirundo fulva, 136
   pyrrhonota, 135
   rustica, 136
Histrionicus histrionicus, 33
Hoopoe, 117
Hummingbird, Allen's, 116
   Anna's 114
   Berylline, 112
   Black-chinned, 114
   Blue-throated, 113
   Broad-billed, 111
   Broad-tailed, 115
   Buff-bellied, 112
   Bumblebee, 115
   Calliope, 115
   Costa's, 115
   Lucifer, 114
   Magnificent, 113
   Ruby-throated, 114
   Rufous, 116
   Rufous-tailed, 112
   Violet-crowned, 112
   White-eared, 111
Hydrobates pelagicus, 10
Hydrobatidae, 9
Hylocharis leucotis, 111
Hylocichla mustelina, 153

Ibis, Glossy, 21
   Scarlet, 21
   White, 20
   White-faced, 21
Icteria virens, 180
Icterus cucullatus, 202
   galbula, 204
   graduacauda, 203
   gularis, 203
   parisorum, 204
   pectoralis, 203
   pustulatus, 203
   spurius, 202
   wagleri, 202

Ictinia mississippiensis, 39
Ixobrychus exilis, 17
Ixoreus naevius, 155

Jabiru, 22
Jabiru mycteria, 22
Jacana, Northern, 61
Jacana spinosa, 61
Jacanidae, 61
Jaeger, Long-tailed, 77
   Parasitic, 77
   Pomarine, 77
Jay, Blue, 137
   Brown, 137
   Gray, 136
   Gray-breasted, 138
   Green, 137
   Pinyon, 138
   Scrub, 138
   Stellar's, 137
Junco hyemalis, 195
   phaeonotus, 195
Junco, Dark-eyed, 195
   Yellow-eyed, 195
Jynx torquilla, 118

Kestrel, American 45
   Eurasian, 45
Killdeer, 59
Kingbird, Cassin's, 130
   Couch's, 130
   Eastern, 131
   Gray, 131
   Loggerhead, 132
   Thick-billed, 131
   Tropical, 130
   Western, 131
Kingfisher, Belted, 117
   Green, 117
   Ringed, 117
Kinglet, Golden-crowned , 149
   Ruby-crowned, 149
Kiskadee, Great, 129
Kite, American Swallow-tailed, 38
   Black-shouldered, 38

Hook-billed, 38
Mississippi, 39
Snail, 39
Kittiwake, Black-legged, 83
Red-legged, 83
Knot, Great, 69
Red, 69

Lagopus lagopus, 48
    mutus, 48
Lampornis clemenciae, 113
Lanius cristatus, 162
    excubitor, 162
    ludovicianus, 163
Laniidae, 162
Lapwing, Northern, 57
Laridae, 77
Lark, Horned, 133
Larus argentatus, 80
    articulla, 78
    californicus, 80
    canus, 79
    delawarensis, 80
    fuscus, 81
    glaucescens, 82
    glaucoides, 81
    heermanni, 79
    hyperboreus, 82
    livens, 81
    marinus, 82
    minutus, 78
    occidentalis, 82
    philadelphia, 79
    pipixcan, 78
    ridibundus, 79
    schistisagus, 81
    thayeri, 80
Laterallus jamaicensis, 52
Leptotila verreauxi, 97
Leucosticte arctoa, 205
Limicola falcinellus, 74
Limnodromus griseus, 74
    scolopaceus, 75
Limnothlypis swainsonii, 175
Limosa fedoa, 68

haemastica, 67
lapponica, 67
limosa, 67
Limpkin, 55
Locustella ochotensis, 148
Logopus leucurus, 49
Longspur, Chestnut-collared, 196
    Lapland, 196
    McCown's, 196
    Smith's, 196
Loon, Arctic, 2
    Common, 2
    Red-throated, 2
    Yellow-billed, 2
Lophodytes cucullatus, 36
Loxia curvirostra, 206
    leucoptera, 206
Luscinia calliope, 151
    svecica, 151
Lymnocryptes minimus, 75

Magpie, Black-billed, 139
    Yellow-billed, 139
Mallard, 28
Martin, Common House-, 136
    Cuban, 133
    Gray-breasted, 134
    Purple, 133
    Southern, 134
Meadowlark, Eastern, 199
    Western, 200
Melanerpes aurifrons, 119
    carolinus, 119
    erythrocephalus, 118
    formicivorus, 118
    lewis, 118
    uropygialis, 119
Melanitta fusca, 34
    nigra, 34
    perspicillata, 34
Meleagris gallopavo, 50
Melopsittacus undulatus, 97
Melospiza georgiana, 194
    lincolnii, 194
    melodia, 193

Merganser, Common, 36
    Hooded, 36
    Red-breasted, 36
Mergus merganser, 36
    serrator, 36
Merlin, 45
Micrathene whitneyi, 104
Mimidae, 156
Mimus gundlachii, 156
    polyglottos, 156
Mniotilta varia, 174
Mockingbird, Bahama, 156
    Northern, 156
Molothrus aeneus, 201
    ater, 202
Moorhen, Common, 54
Motacilla alba, 159
    cinerea, 159
    flava, 159
    lugens, 160
Motacillidae, 159
Murre, Common, 89
    Thick-billed, 89
Murrelet, Ancient, 91
    Craveri's, 91
    Kittlitz's, 90
    Marbled, 90
    Xantus', 90
Muscicapa griseisticta, 150
    sibirica, 150
Muscicapidae, 147
Myadestes townsendi, 152
Mycteria americana, 22
Myiarchus cinerascens, 128
    crinitus, 128
    sagrae, 129
    tuberculifer, 128
    tyrannulus, 129
Myioborus miniatus, 179
    pictus, 179
Myiodynastes luteiventris, 129
Myna, Crested, 163
Myopsitta monachus, 98

Needletail, White-throated, 109

Neocrex erythrops, 54
Nighthawk, Antillean, 107
    Common, 106
    Lesser, 106
Nightjar, Buff-collared, 108
    Jungle, 108
Noddy, Black, 88
    Brown, 88
Nucifraga columbiana, 138
Numenius americanus, 67
    arquata, 66
    borealis, 65
    madagascariensis, 66
    minutus, 65
    phaeopus, 65
    tahitiensis, 66
    tenuirostris, 66
Nutcracker, Clark's, 138
Nuthatch, Brown-headed, 144
    Pygmy, 144
    Red-breasted, 144
    White-breasted, 144
Nyctea scandiaca, 103
Nycticorax nycticorax, 20
    violaceus, 20
Nyctidromus albicollis, 107

Oceanites oceanicus, 9
Oceanodroma castro, 11
    furcata, 10
    homochroa, 11
    leucorhoa, 10
    melania, 11
    microsoma, 12
    tethys, 11
Oenanthe oenanthe, 151
Oldsquaw, 34
Oporornis agilis, 177
    formosus, 176
    philadelphia, 177
    tolmiei, 177
Oreortyx pictus, 52
Oreoscoptes montanus, 157
Oriole, Altamire, 203
    Audubon's, 203

Black-vented, 202
Hooded, 202
Northern, 204
Orchard, 202
Scott's, 204
Spot-breasted, 203
Streak-backed, 203
Ortalis vetula, 46
Osprey, 38
Otus asio, 102
    flammeolus, 102
    kennicottii, 102
    sunia, 101
    trichopsis, 102
Ovenbird, 176
Owl, Barred, 105
    Boreal, 106
    Burrowing, 104
    Common Barn-, 101
    Eastern Screech-, 102
    Elf, 104
    Ferruginous Pygmy-, 104
    Flammulated, 102
    Great Gray, 105
    Great Horned, 103
    Long-eared, 105
    Northern Hawk-, 103
    Northern Saw-whet, 106
    Northern Pygmy-, 103
    Oriental Scops-, 101
    Short-eared, 105
    Snowy, 103
    Spotted, 104
    Western Screech-, 102
    Whiskered Screech-, 102
Oxyura dominica, 37
    jamaicensis, 36
Oystercatcher, American, 60
    American Black, 60

Pachyramphus aglaiae, 132
Pagophila eburnea, 84
Pandion haliaetus, 38
Parabuteo unicinctus, 41
Parakeet, Canary-winged, 98

Monk, 98
Rose-ringed, 98
Pardirallus maculatus, 54
Paridae, 141
Parrot, Red-crowned, 99
    Thick-billed, 98
    Yellow-headed, 99
Partirdge, Gray, 47
Parula americana, 168
    pitiayumi, 169
Parula, Northern, 168
    Tropical, 169
Parus atricapillus, 141
    bicolor, 143
    carolinensis, 141
    cinctus, 142
    gambeli, 141
    hudsonicus, 142
    inornatus, 143
    rufescens, 142
    sclateri, 141
    wollweberi, 142
Passer domesticus, 209
    montanus, 209
Passerculus sandwichensis, 191
Passerella iliaca, 193
Passeridae, 209
Passerina amoena, 184
    ciris, 185
    cyanea, 184
    versicolor, 185
Pauraque, Common, 107
Pelagodroma marina, 10
Pelecanidae, 14
Pelecanus erythrorhynchos, 14
    occidentalis, 14
Pelican, American White, 14
    Brown, 14
Perdix perdix, 47
Perisoreus canadensis, 136
Petrel, Black-capped, 6
    Mottled, 6
Peucedramus taeniatus, 180
Pewee, Eastern Wood-, 124
    Greater, 124

Western Wood-, 124
Phaethon aethereus, 12
   lepturus, 12
   rubricauda, 12
Phaethontidae, 12
Phainopepla, 162
Phainopepla nitens, 162
Phalacrocoracidae, 14
Phalacrocorax auritus, 15
   carbo, 14
   olivaceus, 15
   pelagicus, 15
   penicillatus, 15
   urile, 16
Phalaenoptilus nuttallii, 107
Phalarope, Red, 76
   Red-necked, 76
   Wilson's, 76
Phalaropus fulicaria, 76
   lobatus, 76
   tricolor, 76
Phasianidae, 47
Phasianus colchicus, 47
Pheasant, Ring-necked, 47
Pheucticus chrysopeplus, 183
   ludovicianus, 183
   melanocephalus, 183
Philomachus pugnax, 74
Phoebe, Black, 127
   Eastern, 127
   Say's, 127
Phoenicopteridae, 22
Phoenicopterus ruber, 22
Phylloscopus borealis, 148
   fuscatus, 148
   sibilatrix, 148
Pica nuttalli, 139
   pica, 139
Picidae, 118
Picoides albolarvatus, 122
   arcticus, 122
   borealis, 121
   nuttallii, 120
   pubescens, 121
   scalaris, 120

   stricklandi, 121
   tridactylus, 122
   villosus, 121
Pigeon, Band-tailed, 94
   Red-billed 94
   Scaly-naped, 94
   White-crowned, 94
Pinicola enucleator, 205
Pintail, Northern, 29
   White-cheeked, 28
Pipilo aberti, 186
   chlorurus, 186
   erythrophthalmus, 186
   fuscus, 186
Pipit, Brown Tree-, 160
   Olive Tree-, 160
   Pechora, 160
   Red-throated, 161
   Sprague's, 161
   Water, 161
Piranga flava, 181
   ludovinciana, 182
   olivacea, 182
   rubra, 181
Pitangus suphuratus, 129
Plectrophenax hyperboreus, 198
   nivalis, 198
Plegadis chihi, 21
   falcinellus, 21
Plover, Black-bellied, 57
   Common Ringed, 58
   Greater Golden, 57
   Lesser Golden, 57
   Little Ringed, 59
   Mongolian, 58
   Mountain, 60
   Piping, 59
   Semipalmated, 59
   Snowy, 58
   Wilson's, 58
Pluvialis apricaria, 57
   dominica, 57
   squatarola, 57
Pochard, Common, 31
Podiceps auritus, 3

grisegena, 3
nigricollis, 4
Podicipedidae, 3
Podilymbus podiceps, 3
Polioptila caerulea, 149
melanura, 149
nigriceps, 150
Polyborus plancus, 44
Polysticta stelleri, 33
Pooecetes gramineus, 190
Poorwill, Common, 107
Porphyrula martinica, 54
Porzana carolina, 53
Prairie-Chicken, Greater, 49
Lesser, 50
Procellariidae, 6
Progne chalybea, 134
cryptoleuca, 133
elegans, 134
subis, 133
Protonotaria citrea, 175
Prunella montanella, 159
Prunellidae, 159
Psaltriparus minimus, 143
Psittacidae, 97
Psittacula krameri, 98
Ptarmigan, Rock, 48
White-tailed, 49
Willow, 48
Pterodroma hasitata, 6
inexpectata, 6
Ptilogonatidae, 162
Ptychoramphys aleuticus, 91
Puffin, Atlantic, 93
Horned, 93
Tufted, 93
Puffinus assimilis, 9
bulleri, 8
carneipes, 7
creatopus, 7
gravis, 7
griseus, 8
iherminieri, 9
opisthomelas, 9
puffinus, 8

tenuirostris, 8
Pycnonotidae, 145
Pycnonotus jocosus, 145
Pyrocephalus rubinus, 128
Pyrrhula pyrrhula, 208
Pyrrhuloxia, 183

Quail, California, 51
Gambel's, 51
Montezuma, 50
Mountain, 52
Scaled, 51
Quiscalus major, 201
mexicanus, 201
quiscula, 201

Rail, black 52
Clapper, 53
King, 53
Spotted, 54
Virginia, 53
Yellow, 52
Rallidae, 52
Rallus elegans, 53
limicola, 53
longirostris, 53
Raven, Chihuahuan, 140
Common, 140
Razorbill, 89
Recurvirostra americana, 61
Recurvirostridae, 61
Redhead, 31
Redpoll, Common, 207
Hoary, 207
Redshank, Spotted, 62
Redstart, American, 175
Painted, 179
Slated-throated, 179
Regulus calendula, 149
satrapa, 149
Remizidae, 143
Rhodostethia rosea, 83
Rhodothraupus celaeno, 182
Rhynchopsitta pachyrhyncha, 98
Ridgwayia pinicola, 155

Riparia riparia, 135

Rissa brevirostris, 83

   tridactyla, 83

Roadrunner, Greater, 100

Robin, American, 155

   Clay-colored, 154

   Rufous-backed, 155

Rosefinch, common, 205

Rostrhamus sociabilis, 39

Rubythroat, Siberian, 151

Ruff, 74

Rynchops niger, 88

Salpinctes obsoletus, 145

Sanderling, 69

Sandpiper, Baird's, 71

   Broad-billed, 74

   Buff-breasted, 74

   Common, 64

   Curlew, 73

   Least, 71

   Marsh, 62

   Pectoral, 72

   Purple, 72

   Rock, 72

   Semipalmated, 69

   Sharp-tailed, 72

   Solitary, 63

   Spoonbill, 73

   Spotted, 64

   Stilt, 73

   Terek, 64

   Upland, 65

   Western, 70

   White-rumped, 71

   Wood, 63

Sapsucker, Red-breasted, 120

   Williamson's, 120

   Yellow-bellied, 119

Sayornis nigricans, 127

   phoebe, 127

   saya, 127

Scaup, Greater, 32

   Lesser, 32

Scolopacidae, 61

Scolopax minor, 76

   rusticola, 75

Scoter, Black, 34

   Surf, 34

   White-winged, 34

Seedeater, White-collared, 187

Seiurus aurocapillus, 176

   motacilla, 176

   noveboracensis, 176

Selasphorus platycercus, 115

   rufus, 116

   sasin, 116

Setophaga ruticilla, 175

Shearwater, Audubon's, 9

   Black-vented, 9

   Buller's, 8

   Cory's, 7

   Flesh-footed, 7

   Greater, 7

   Little, 9

   Manx, 8

   Pink-footed, 7

   Short-tailed, 8

   Sooty, 8

   Streaked, 6

Shoveler, Northern, 30

Shrike, Brown, 162

   Loggerhead, 163

   Northern, 162

Sialia currucoides, 152

   mexicana, 152

   sialis, 151

Siskin, Pine, 207

Sitta canadensis, 144

   carolinensis, 144

   pusilla, 144

   pygmaea, 144

Sittidae, 144

Skimer, Black, 88

Skua, Great, 77

   South Polar, 78

Skylark, Eurasian, 133

Smew, 35

Snipe, Common, 75

   Jack, 75

Solitaire, Townsend's 152
Somateria fischeri, 33
    mollissima, 32
    spectabilis, 33
Sora, 53
Sparrow, American Tree, 188
    Bachman's, 187
    Baird's, 192
    Black-chinned, 190
    Black-throated, 190
    Botteri's, 187
    Brewer's, 189
    Cassin's, 188
    Chipping, 189
    Clay-colored, 189
    Eurasian Tree, 209
    Field, 189
    Five-striped, 191
    Fox, 193
    Golden-crowned, 194
    Grasshopper, 192
    Harris', 195
    Henslow's, 192
    House, 209
    Lark, 190
    Le Conte's, 192
    Lincoln's, 194
    Olive, 185
    Rufous-crowned, 188
    Rufous-winged, 188
    Sage, 191
    Savannah, 191
    Seaside, 193
    Sharp-tailed, 193
    Song, 193
    Swamp, 194
    Vesper, 190
    White-crowned, 195
    White-throated, 194
Sphyrapicus ruber, 120
    thuroideus, 120
    varius, 119
Spindalis zena, 181
Spiza americana, 185
Spizella arborea, 188

    atrogularis, 190
    breweri, 189
    pallida, 189
    passerina, 189
    pusilla, 189
Spoonbill, Roseate, 21
Sporophila torqueola, 187
Starling, European, 163
Starthroat, Plain-capped, 113
Stelgidopteryx serripennis, 135
Stellula calliope, 115
Stercorarius longicaudus, 77
    parasiticus, 77
    pomarinus, 77
Sterna aleutica, 86
    anaethetus, 87
    antillarum, 86
    caspia, 84
    dougallii, 85
    elegans, 85
    forsteri, 86
    fuscata, 87
    hirundo, 85
    maxima, 84
    nilotica, 84
    paradisaea, 86
    sandvicensis, 85
Stilt, Black-necked, 61
Stint, Little, 70
    Long-toed, 71
    Rufous-necked, 70
    Temminck's, 70
Stork, Wood, 22
Storm-Petrel, Ashy, 11
    Band-rumped, 11
    Black, 11
    British, 10
    Fork-tailed, 10
    Leach's, 10
    Least, 12
    Wedge-rumped, 11
    White-faced, 10
    Wilson's, 9
Streptopelia chinensis, 95
    risoria, 95

Streptoprocne zonaris, 109
Strigidae, 101
Strix nebulosa, 105
   occidentalis, 104
   varia, 105
Sturnella magna, 199
   neglecta, 200
Sturnidae, 163
Sturnus vulgaris, 163
Sula bassanus, 14
   datylatra, 13
   leucogaster, 13
   nebouxii, 13
   sula, 13
Sulidae, 13
Surfbird, 68
Surnia ulula, 103
Swallow, Bahama, 135
   Bank, 135
   Barn, 136
   Cave, 136
   Cliff, 135
   Northern Rough-winged, 135
   Tree, 134
   Violet-green, 134
Swan, Mute, 24
   Trumpeter, 23
   Tundra, 23
   Whooper, 23
Swift, Antillean Palm, 100
   Black, 108
   Chimney, 109
   Common, 110
   Fork-tailed, 110
   Vaux's, 109
   White-collared, 109
   White-throated, 110
Synthliboramphus antiquus, 91
   craveri, 91
   hypoleucus, 90

Tachornis phoenicobia, 110
Tachybaptus dominicus, 3
Tachycineta bicolor, 134
   cyaneoviridis, 135

   thalassina, 134
Tanager, Hepatic, 181
   Scarlet, 182
   Stripe-headed, 181
   Summer, 181
   Western, 182
Tattler, Gray-tailed, 64
   Wandering, 63
Teal, Baikal, 27
   Blue-winged, 29
   Cinnamon, 29
   Falcated, 27
   Green-winged, 27
Tern, Aleutian, 86
   Arctic, 86
   Black, 87
   Bridled, 87
   Caspian, 84
   Common, 85
   Elegant, 85
   Forster's, 86
   Gull-billed, 84
   Least, 86
   Roseate, 85
   Royal, 84
   Sandwich, 85
   Sooty, 87
   White-winged, 87
Thick-knee, Double-striped, 56
Thrasher, Bendire's, 157
   Brown, 157
   California, 158
   Crissal, 158
   Curve-billed, 158
   Le Conte's, 158
   Long-billed, 157
   Sage, 157
Threskiornithidae, 20
Thrush, Aztec, 155
   Dusky, 154
   Eye-browed, 154
   Gray-cheeked, 153
   Hermit, 153
   Swainson's, 153
   Varied, 155

Wood, 153
Thryomanes bewickii, 146
Thryothorus ludovicianus, 146
Tiaris bicolor, 187
Tit, Siberian, 142
Titmouse, Bridled, 142
    Plain, 143
    Tufted, 143
Towhee, Abert's, 186
    Brown, 186
    Green-tailed, 186
    Rufous-sided, 186
Toxostoma bendirei, 157
    curvirostre, 158
    dorsale, 158
    lecontei, 158
    longirostre, 157
    redivivum, 158
    rufum, 157
Tringa erythropus, 62
    flavipes, 62
    glareola, 63
    melanoleuca, 62
    nebularia, 61
    solitaria, 63
    stagnatilis, 62
Trochilidae, 111
Troglodytes aedon, 146
    troglodytes, 147
Troglodytidae, 145
Trogon elegans, 116
Trogon, Eared, 116
    Elegant, 116
Trogonidae, 116
Tropicbird, Red-billed, 12
    Red-tailed, 12
    White-tailed, 12
Tryngites subruficollis, 74
Turdus grayi, 154
    migratorius, 155
    naumanni, 154
    obscurus, 154
    pilaris, 154
    rufopalliatus, 155
Turkey, Wild, 50

Turnstone, Black, 68
    Ruddy, 68
Tympanuchus cupido, 49
    pallidicinctus, 50
    phasianellus, 50
Tyrannidae, 123
Tyrannulet, Northern Beardless-, 123
Tyrannus caudifasciatus, 132
    couchii, 130
    crassirostris, 131
    dominicensis, 131
    forficatus, 132
    melancholicus, 130
    savana, 132
    tyrannus, 131
    verticalis, 131
    vociferans, 130
Tyto alba, 101
Tytonidae, 101

Upupa epops, 117
Upupidae, 117
Uria aalge, 89
    lomvia, 89

Vanellus vanellus, 57
Veery, 152
Verdin, 143
Vermivora bachmanii, 166
    celata, 167
    chrysoptera, 167
    crissalis, 168
    luciae, 168
    peregrina, 167
    pinus, 166
    ruficapilla, 167
    superciliosa, 169
    virginiae, 168
Violet-ear, Green, 111
Vireo altiloquus, 166
    atricapillus, 164
    bellii, 164
    flavifrons, 165
    gilvus, 165
    griseus, 163

huttoni, 165
olivaceus, 166
philadelphicus, 165
solitarius, 164
vicinior, 164
Vireo, Bell's, 164
Black-capped, 164
Black-whiskered, 166
Gray, 164
Hutton's, 165
Philadelphia, 165
Red-eyed, 166
Solitary, 164
Warbling, 165
White-eyed, 163
Yellow-throated, 165
Vireonidae, 163
Vulture, Black, 37
Turkey, 37

Wagtail, Black-backed, 160
Gray, 159
White, 159
Yellow, 159
Warbler, Arctic, 148
Bachman's, 166
Bay-breasted, 174
Black-and-white, 174
Black-throated Blue, 170
Black-throated Gray, 171
Black-throated Green, 171
Blackburnian, 172
Blackpoll, 174
Blue-winged, 166
Canada, 178
Cape May, 170
Cerulean, 174
Chestnut-sided, 169
Colima, 168
Connecticut, 177
Crescent-chested, 169
Dusky, 148
Fan-tailed, 179
Golden-cheeked, 172
Golden-crowned, 180

Golden-winged, 167
Grace's, 172
Hermit, 171
Hooded, 178
Kentucky, 176
Kirtland's, 173
Lucy's, 168
MacGillivray's, 177
Magnolia, 170
Middendorf's Grasshopper, 148
Mourning, 177
Nashville, 167
Olive, 180
Orange-crowned, 167
Palm, 173
Pine, 173
Prairie, 173
Prothonotary, 175
Red-faced, 179
Rufous-capped, 180
Swainson's, 175
Tennessee, 167
Townsend's, 171
Virginia's, 168
Wilson's, 178
Wood, 148
Worm-eating, 175
Yellow, 169
Yellow-rumped, 170
Yellow-throated, 172
Waterthrush, Louisiana, 176
Northern, 176
Waxwing, Bohemian, 161
Cedar, 162
Wheatear, Northern, 151
Whimbrel, 65
Whip-poor-will, 108
Wigeon, American, 30
Eurasian, 30
Willet, 63
Wilsonia canadensis, 178
citrina, 178
pusilla, 178
Woodcock, American 76
Eurasian, 75

Woodpecker, Acorn, 118
Black-backed, 122
Downy, 121
Gila, 119
Golden-fronted, 119
Hairy, 121
Ivory-billed, 123
Ladder-backed, 120
Lewis', 118
Nuttall's, 120
Pileated, 123
Red-bellied, 119
Red-cockaded, 121
Red-headed, 118
Strickland's, 121
Three-toed, 122
White-headed, 122
Woodstar, Bahama, 113
Wren, Bewick's, 146
Cactus, 145
Canyon, 146
Carolina, 146
House, 146
Marsh, 147
Rock, 145
Sedge, 147
Winter, 147
Wrentit, 156
Wryneck, Eurasian, 118

Xanthocephalus xanthocephalus, 200
Xema sabini, 83
Xenus cinereus, 64

Yellowlegs, Greater, 62
Lesser, 62
Yellowthroat, Common, 177
Gray-crowned, 178

Zenaida asiatica, 95
aurita, 95
macroura, 96
Zonotrichia albicollis, 194
atricapilla, 194
leucophrys, 195
querula, 195

To order additional copies of *Pocket Life List*:

Web: www.itascabooks.com
Phone: 1-800-901-3480
Fax: Copy and fill out the form below with credit card information.
        Fax to 651-603-9263.
Mail: Copy and fill out the form below. Mail with check or credit
        card information to: Syren Book Company, 2402 University
        Avenue West, Saint Paul, Minnesota 55114

Order Form

Copies	Title / Author	Price	Totals	
	Pocket Life List / Fashingbauer	$16.95	$	
		Subtotal	$	
		7% sales tax (MN only)	$	
		Shipping and handling, first copy	$	4.00
		Shipping and handling, ___ add'l copies @$1.00 ea.	$	
		TOTAL TO REMIT	$	

Payment Information

__ Check Enclosed __ Visa/Mastercard		
Card number:	Expiration date:	
Name on card:		
Billing address:		
City:	State:	Zip:
Signature :	Date:	

Shipping Information

__ Same as billing address __ Other (enter below)		
Name:		
Address:		
City:	State:	Zip: